Boat Fishing
at Sea

Boat Fishing at Sea

PHILL WILLIAMS & BRIAN DOUGLAS

Beekay Publishers

Other angling titles by Beekay Publishers:

Sea

Uptide & Boatcasting by Bob Cox
Long Range Casting & Fishing Techniques by Paul Kerry
Cod Fishing by John Rawle

Coarse

Carp Fever by Kevin Maddocks
Success with the Pole by Dickie Carr
Pike Fishing in the 80's by Neville Fickling
Basic Carp Fishing by Peter Mohan
Modern Specimen Hunting by Jim Gibbinson
Fishing for Big Chub by Peter Stone
Top Ten – tactics for the major species by ten leading
specialist anglers. Edited by Bruce Vaughan
Redmire Pool by Kevin Clifford & Len Arbery
Tactics for Big Pike by Bill Chillingworth
In Pursuit of Carp & Catfish by Kevin Maddocks
Cypry The Carp by Peter Mohan
The Beekay Guide to Carp Waters
Jim Davidson Gets Hooked by Jim Davidson
In Pursuit of Predatory Fish by Neville Fickling
Tiger Bay by Rob Maylin
Understanding Barbel by Fred Crouch
Big-Water Carp by Jim Gibbinson
Mega-Pike by Eddie Turner

Game

The Colour Guide to Fly Tying by Kevin Hyatt
Robson's Guide – Stillwater Trout Flies. An Alphabetical
Survey in Colour by Kenneth Robson
Dressed to Kill by Bob Carnill & Kenneth Robson

First published in 1984
Reprinted 1990
BEEKAY PUBLISHERS
WITHY POOL
HENLOW CAMP
BEDS. SG16 6EA
ENGLAND

ISBN 0 947674 26 8

Produced by Castle Cary Press, Somerset

CONTENTS

Foreword

Small boat fishing is an unusually difficult topic in that it involves the very careful marrying together of two normally divorced subjects. Not only must there be an ability to locate fish by one's own devices, but this must be done with a degree of skill and competence at the helm. For this reason, Phill Williams and Brian Douglas have pooled their assorted talents to offer what must be the single most comprehensive and objective look at this ever growing aspect of the sport of angling.

Although for ease of presentation *Boat Fishing at Sea* might look like one man's views on the subject, it is in fact a carefully blended amalgam of experiences. As an experienced angling journalist, Phill Williams set out the words in print, while Brian Douglas double checked, researched and typed up the final draft. Throughout, every endeavour has been made to offer sound, well reasoned advice leaving no stone unturned. This passion for total accuracy is reflected in the accompanying illustrations from the pen and camera of Phill Williams which combine with the text to produce a work that goes deeper into the subject than any other previous publication.

Both Phill Williams and Brian Douglas are equally as expert with the rod as they are with the written word, and they have a huge list of catches and specimen dinghy-caught fish which illustrates their expertise. Brian's best cod weighed 31lbs 10oz, for example, and he once caught three cod, each well over 20lbs, in consecutive outings. Phill has taken a tope of 50lbs, and has also held three national records — for mullet, tub gurnard and spotted ray. Consistently successful fishing comes from a special grasp of the situation at hand and this quality emanates from every page of this book.

The authors – Phill Williams (left) and Brian Douglas.

Personal Dossiers

Born in Liverpool in 1948, Phill Williams moved with his parents to his current home town of Leyland, Lancs in 1956, where he developed a love for coarse fishing in the company of his new school friends, culminating in a Duke of Edinburgh Award with angling as his hobby. Then, like so many young chaps entering their teens, his attention was caught by other attractions, and it was not until 1970 when he finally married Brenda that fishing again found a place in his life, although he stresses at this point that it was not married life that drove him to it. This time it was to be sea fishing, and very quickly, small boat fishing, under the guidance of one particular Scottish character called Davy Agnew. Later, as the glitter of 450 mile round trips began to wear thin, his attentions turned to his home stretch, the Fylde coast, in the company of Keith Philbin and Mick Mairs. Not that sea fishing is his only love: certain aspects of game fishing also make their demands, in particular char and schelly, which nudged him into studying freshwater fishery management techniques to examination level with the Institute of Fisheries Management. Phill now has two children, Ian and Dawn, both of whom fish, in particular Ian who is closely following in dad's wake, which will become apparent as the book unfolds.

Born in Preston in 1951, Brian Douglas started fishing around the age of five under the watchful eye of father Bob, doing the rounds of local farm ponds for roach and rudd. As time marched on, the call of the sea began to take precedence. At first it was to the Fylde coast piers, but that only satisfied his enthusiasm for so long. The pair then joined a local boat angling club before settling into the challenge of finding their own fish as and when they liked. Brian also married a Brenda in 1972 and has three children, the two eldest of which are boys to keep the tradition of fishing in the Douglas family alive and well. Brian too is fast developing an interest in angling photography, although he stresses that his major involvement will always be with the practical side.

SECTION ONE

GOING AFLOAT

What to buy

More sea anglers than ever are now turning their thoughts towards putting to sea on their own. Dinghy fishing, is, metaphorically speaking, riding on the crest of a wave, and therein lies the ultimate opportunity to step into the skipper's wellies, or in this case waders, assuming all the control that goes with it. On the other hand as they say, perhaps the grass only looks greener from the other side, for the reality of the thing is that out there you will have no other feet at which to lay the blame should the fishing, or worse still, the weather take a turn for the worse. It is at such times as these that the man on the tiller may truly command his own destiny. Rewards can be high, with the added bonus of self satisfaction in achievement totally by your own efforts. Risks too may come in doses of equal measure. I bet few prospective dinghy converts, on entering the buying market, consider even in passing just exactly what they might be letting themselves in for. What is to come in this opening section could well prove a little off putting. What a lot of interested parties often fail to appreciate is that we are talking here of an amalgam of two quite distinct branches of interest. Catching fish is all very well, but without competency in boat handling, it is not much good. To glamorise the whole thing in order to win a few converts is just not sensible. Out there, it can be risky, weary, miserable hard work. It can also be the most entertaining, stimulating and personally self satisfying pastime I know. You have to take the rough with the smooth. Handling the rough is what this section is all about. The smooth comes in section two, and I wouldn't change any of it for the world.

Just a simple word of warning, particularly for prospective first time buyers; that compelling urge for boat ownership often drives out any measure of common sense, often resulting in the buying of the wrong boat for the job. Before leaving home armed with a pocket full of pound notes, pause for a moment and think. Are you up to all that physical hard work, frustration, additional unforeseen cost, problems, and above all dangers? Suddenly you will be out there fishing with even less of a guarantee than the most pessimistic charter skipper might care to offer. Motoring over that vast expanse of featureless emptiness, the pathway to success must be one of your own plotting.

Where many newcomers become disillusioned is in failing to realise just how little time, despite long periods away from home, is actually spent dangling a bait. Ideas of a quick burst out leading to a bag full of fish are for the bedtime hours, with little chance of ever becoming reality. If it is 'no hassle fishing' that turns you on, stick with the charter boats where all the preparation, fish finding, trouble shooting and cleaning up afterwards is catered for in the fee. Very often, less than half the time involved will be spent trying to catch fish. Taking weather reports, weighing up the best tides, gathering bait, preparing tackle, loading up, collecting the crew, travelling, launching, dumping the trailer and finally sailing out consumes great portions of the day. Then the whole thing has to be reversed, with time added on for tidying up before the boat goes away; at least that is how a proper trip is organised. Many, in fact, are not, the result being that sooner or later those of us obeying all the rules end up with a portion of any collective dressing down being banded about. So far as dinghy fishing goes, there are no laws in Britain as yet concerning who can or cannot put to sea in a small private boat. Should you decide to kill yourself, the coastguard can do little more than stand there complaining bitterly. A harbour master has the right to prevent you using his facilities, but no power to prevent your drowning elsewhere. It is good to be free from binding restrictions, providing we are seen to be for the most part responsibly excercising these rights. As more pressure is put on emergency and rescue services to bail the irresponsible element out, that time is fast approaching when, due to the actions of the few, the many may have to prove their competence, and be required by law to undergo some sort of licensing check.

Allow me to quote from *Angling Times*: a R.N.L.I. spokesman complained, and rightly so, that in 1982, lifeboats had been summoned to 252 small boats, a great many of which carried anglers. In all, 11 persons died — 5 due to capsizes, while 4 fell overboard and died as a result of swampings. Half the incidents in question took place after dark. Sad though such accidents are, it infuriates me that innocent as I am, along with many hundreds of other boaters, I will be tarred by the same brush destined eventually to sweep in legislative changes. The aim then of this book is to cut out the need for legally enforced care at sea, hopefully with a few more fish in the box as reward for doing so.

Let us first define just exactly what a dinghy is. Generally speaking, it encompasses all that is small and floats, with either trailing or roof rack mobility as required. Few people in the sea angling arena seem willing to be be more precise, which forces us to do so in this book. For safe, comfortable regular sea fishing outings, if you put to sea in anything capable of being transported on a car roof, inflatables included, expect no sympathy for whatever predicament you may find yourself in.

It is people like that who threaten things for the rest of us. As boats are now built in metric as well as imperial sizes, to quote precise figures is difficult; not that we intend to shirk this responsibility but this is just our way of explaining away the need for a little realistic flexibility. We both belong to an organised tractor launching set up known as the Wyre Boat Angling Club, whose constitution is cleverly geared around individual freedom without putting safety in jeopardy. Our upward and downward limits are 16½ and 10 feet respectively. With so many boats now exceeding the once-thought-perfect 16 foot barrier by a fraction, our 16½ foot upper limit seemed the only realistic way to avoid upsets or rule bending. A 17 foot boat is one hell of a lump to shift across an open beach, even with a tractor. At the other extreme, ten feet to my way of thinking is an invitation to trouble. Even on a mirror calm day, the only regular body movement you can indulge in with

A typical fast planing hull, but at 18 feet too big for regular beach launching.

safety is side-to-side eye-ball juggling! Fortunately, our seventy boat membership appear to have had similar thoughts. If I thought a ten foot boat was my only access to the sea, I would pack up fishing, lash the thing to my window ledge, drill a few drain holes in the bottom and take up window box gardening. I am very reluctant to go afloat in anything under 13 feet long. For me, the nearer to 16 feet the better. That additional bit of length may not sound a lot, but length is not the only dimension to benefit. The hull gains beam (width) and freeboard (height above the waterline), creating a much more stable seaworthy package.

Ultimate boat choice and size is affected by a number of factors including launching conditions, weight, and, as important a consideration as any, how the project is to be financed. This is not so much a case of how much cash you can scrape up or borrow, which is a personal matter but it is the category of ownership that may dictate any limitations of size or weight. Several categories of ownership are possible. The first is straightforward enough. Dig deep into your pocket, and providing you can manage a launch on your own, or with whoever you might care to invite along, buy whatever you feel suits you. The other alternatives involve varying degrees of part or shared ownership. Perhaps the one most often entered into is buying everything required, the total cost being split between all parties concerned. Another alternative is teaming up with a fishing friend, or friends, willing to shoulder individual portions of expense and responsibility as part of an organised scheme. For example, one person buys and equips the boat, leaving his mate to come up with the power unit. Both are responsible for the upkeep and maintenance of his particular investment, no matter what the cost incurred, and should a split occur, it leaves two persons either searching for a new partner apiece, or sufficient cash to replace the missing

14

bit. Total cost splitting, while on the face of things looking very much fairer, can be a real problem. Invariably, no single person feels responsible for any upkeep once the novelty has worn off, so nothing gets done. Worse still, should a shareholder decide to take his leave, the rig often ends up on the market to pay him off. This all sounds very mercenary, but group ownership, in that it demands a place on board for every shareholder can narrow the buying market considerably.

When the final figure of persons to be carried is determined, thoughts on matching boat to demands on space can be considered. A working guide starts with a 12 foot hull having a maximum suitability for two persons, moving up in increments of a further two feet per additional person involved. This gives a 16 foot boat a safe carrying capacity of four. Safety, though of paramount importance, is not the only factor if the boat is, as in this case, to be used for angling. Boats with cuddies, large splash wells or extensive buoyancy tanks all eat up fishing space. An open 16 footer will indeed fish four in reasonable comfort, but if you start sticking extras both on it and in it, it won't. I will stick my neck out here and say there is not a dinghy afloat that would not be better off fishing two, with all the rods propped against the stern. This is where a compromise has to be made. How can maximum fishing space be achieved hand in glove with maximum muscle power for getting to and from the water's edge? We used to manhandle our boats across steep shingle and soft sand before the advent of tractors. Making friends with people in a similar position is the only answer. A case of 'you help shove our boat and we'll help to shove yours,' all of which goes to prove that for beach launching, boat size and weight are the limiting factors. To keep your dependency on crew members and other boaters down, a small boat is the answer, yet going too small is an invitation to disaster. Staving off problems while afloat may result in problems actually getting afloat. Dinghy fishing is all about compromise, a word destined for much use. Detailing the full story behind hull design and choice deserves a book all to itself. This is a highly complex subject, even after which each decision would need to be tailored to individual circumstances — all of which points to a bewildering time in store for the first time buyer, who will undoubtedly feel a compelling urgency to put the whole business behind him. Vague advice, as opposed to decisive instruction is all we have to offer; a case of here are the facts, now decide which appertain to you. Without wishing to sound in any way unkind to boat dealers, they should be the last people to be asked for advice, having a vested interest in parting you from your money lest you might take it elsewhere. Given that they had every style of boat to hand, I might be inclined to listen. As they haven't, the less reputable amongst them could try to palm you off with the nearest thing available. Try and resist the sales pitch. If you talk to a cross section of experienced small boat anglers, I can tell you now, even they will not fully agree on the best boat. Where there will be accord is a condemnation of the obvious death traps and problem buys. Most will openly admit to having made mistakes or

Ample room for four in an open 16 footer. With a cuddy, things would be very different.

regrettable buys. If this were not commonplace, why do many require several boats before dropping on the one best suited to their particular needs, which incidentally, will vary from place to place? Your needs will probably differ even from theirs, but what you will be doing is jumping the first few hurdles along the way rather than careering into them.

The perfect boat has not, and never will be designed. With such a vast cross section of features to be aware of, at best your choice will fall into the compromise mould, which is best made by drawing up a list of your particular needs, then matching it as closely as possible to a maker's claims. Primary consideration must be given to how the boat is going to reach the water's edge. If there is a harbour or small creek with adequate mooring facilities, there is no difficulty and your choice is limitless. Moored boats have their own set of drawbacks, the most troublesome being the need for regular pumping out to prevent swamping by rain water. Most dinghies however, come to the water strapped to a vehicle trailer. Concrete slades (launching ramps), running straight into permanent water are almost as good as mooring. Most slades are, to some degree, affected by tide, allowing direct launch or retrieve for only a brief period either side of high water. In these conditions, take care; glass reinforced plastic (GRP or fibre glass), does not take too kindly to being driven against concrete. Sheltered harbours are not too bad as the sea will not be pounding hull against slade. Working just from the concrete means either very short trips of, at most, three to four hours duration even on a big spring tide, or excessively long outings if you decide to fish a tide down and back up again. Ten hour trips sound great in summer or with the fish in suicidal mood; try one in winter, or when after a couple of hours it cuts up rough meaning an eight hour wait to get the boat re-trailered and away. This is why most small boaters think carefully, buying in the knowledge that they must take their rig out onto the

Rare indeed are Slades blessed with water at all stages of the tide.

beach. Open shores vary greatly in their layout. Hard sand with straight-forward access will make things easier for big heavy boats, unlike steep shingle banks, rocky inlets or mud. We have said it before and must stress it again — weight is the single most crucial factor.

Dinghies fall loosely into two main categories — displacement hulls with a large part of their lower region lying below the water surface, based on traditional lines for stability, seaworthiness and comfort, or planing boats with almost the entire hull on top of the water skipping, or planing across the surface, maximising the conversion of engine power into speed. Brian has had several displacement boats but has now switched to a 14 foot planing hull. I too have experience of both, owning a similar planing boat, as well as a 16 foot displacement boat, so we can both talk objectively and without bias. Of course, a number of intermediate hulls are also on the market, the problems and good points of which lean towards the degree of dominance taken from either style. These, would on the face of things seem an obvious choice in that they might offer the best of all worlds. Sadly in practice this has not proved to be the case. No mongrel will ever compete with a thoroughbred, a fact borne out by the refusal of many experienced dinghy owners to entertain semi-displacement boats these days. Some did enjoy a limited measure of success several years ago but have since been alienated by the purist thinkers as misfits in something of a nautical no man's land.

As displacement hulls were traditionally designed first, what better place to start? They are roughly of semi-circular cross section, with pointed bows, their greatest degree of beam (width) lying forward of a mid point, giving way to a gradual taper towards the stern. In terms of maximum beam, they often exceed fast boats. Good beam makes for stability and sea worthiness, but don't run away with the idea that the greater the quoted beam for a displacement hull, the more fishing room it will have over its

An excellent high bowed displacement boat ideally suited to beach launching through surf. Note simulated clinker GRP hull.

Types of Hull

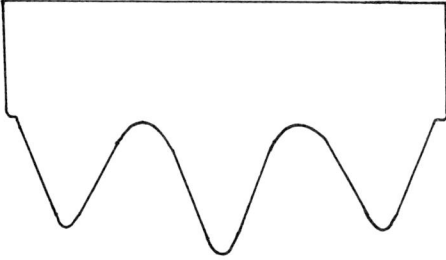

Cathedral hull

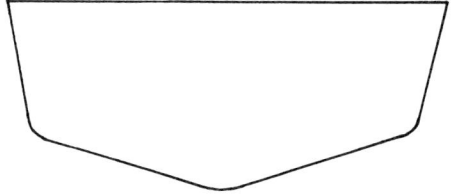

Semi-displacement hull

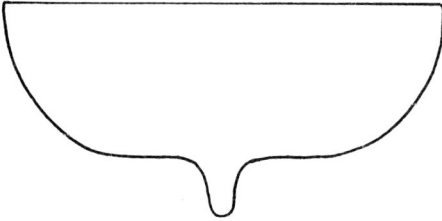

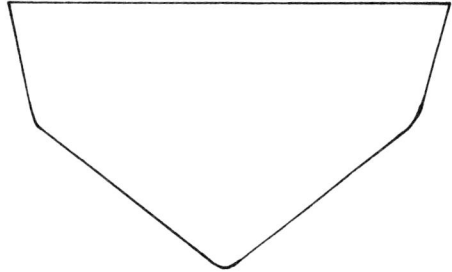

Displacement hull

Deep 'V' hull

rivals, because this may not be so. By the very nature of having both a backward and forward taper from the maximum point, such boats lose a great deal of space. Add to this the curvature of the hull giving rise to quite a narrow deck strip, and actual walking space compared with overall dimensions bears no comparison. Today's hulls more often than not have moulded gunwhales adding much to the boat's overall strength, while at the same time being virtually maintenance free. It may well be that wood is used to trim the hull for strength. Seats also lend much to the overall strength, and while necessary, do much to clutter further the fishing area. You will probably notice that some hulls are smooth while others resemble wood planking. This is called simulated clinker, and is appreciably stronger in design. This range of boats was designed for good handling qualities and safe riding through the water as opposed to skimming along, bounding at the whim of the waves. Their principal drawback is that in displacing water as they go, their top speed is drastically reduced to somewhere in the region of 6 to 8 knots. Clamping a bigger engine on the back will do little other than force the back end deep into the water, or have the nose so high as to become unstable and possibly capsize. Neither Brian nor myself used engines topping ten horse power; these pushed our boats perfectly. A fifteen horse power unit, while not appreciably increasing top speed, would allow a reserve of power to combat head winds or strong tides. Anything more would be ridiculous.

A comparison of the under hull of both styles will show a very striking dis-similarity. Displacement hulls which are semi-circular, rely on keels to dampen side-to-side roll. The degree of keel varies from builder to

Displacement and planing boats at the water's edge. Note how much further in the displacement boat ends up.

builder. Mine has the biggest I have ever come across, which is perfect for leaning over the side and handling in a big sea. But we need to push its trailer into the waves until water reaches the mudguard tops, often getting wet before the day even kicks off. Worse still, it bottoms out miles from the water's edge on the way back in at low water; rolling steeply from side to side as the falling swells remove their support whilst still being amongst biggish waves means we cop a bit of water over the back. It doesn't matter from a safety point of view as we are already ashore. It does however, make life difficult for winching the thing back onto the trailer, particularly with plenty of water inside. Out at sea on a rough day, there is not a boat to touch it for seaworthiness. Always in this game, to gain a good point, something has to be given up in exchange.

I used to criticize planing boats and swore I would not have one under any circumstances. Much of what I said I still stand by, except for the last bit. Though always envious of their speed, the sacrifices called for in order to have it seemed too high a price to pay. I now see things in a somewhat different light, having shared a few trips in Brian's and concede that some of my criticism was a little unjust. Planing boats are to me creatures of two extremes. What it all boils down to is, are their wider range of bad points out-weighed by the many good ones? I now think on balance they probably are, though I would never knock a good displacement boat. Choice should hinge very much on the need , as opposed to the desire for speed, because more often than not, that desire will be kept at bay by conditions. Maintaining peak speed depends entirely on prevailing sea state. It does not take much of a 'lump' to trim this back considerably. For example, when running with even a light swell, by constantly overtaking the peaks, the boat keeps nose slapping into the troughs. Riding into a swell at speed, apart from sending curtains of spray in all directions, sees the boat taking off from the highest point and thumping back down hard. Speed seems best achieved running angled side on to a light swell. Of course, if conditions cut up really rough, it calls for real throttling back to the point where you are just keeping pace with the traditional old plodder, but without any of the benefits he will enjoy.

Fast boats call for big powerful engines. It takes around thirty horse power to bring a 14 foot boat up to full plane. For greater pace, or a reserve of power, you can keep on going all the way up to sixty horse power. Bigger hulls can obviously take even more. Fail to fit a big enough power unit and you end up with all the bad points of flat bottomed boating in exchange for nothing good. Big engines unfortunately create all sorts of headaches in the launching stage. As they are so heavy, it takes more muscle power to manhandle the rig to the water's edge. They are also very thirsty, though in fairness, they require a shorter running time between A and B, so they may not use that much more fuel for a set distance. Where thirst becomes apparent is in making long journeys, to which fast boats are particularly well suited. Full fuel tanks can mean around 50 to 60 pounds of additional weight. A lot of weight also comes with electric start calling for heavy batteries. If manhandling problems arise with a displacement boat, the engine can be removed, but not so in this case. Large motors are bolted in position as well as clamped, and you wouldn't lift it anyway. Bolted engines mean life spent outside in the elements. Another drawback is getting through the shoreline surf to more comfortable water beyond. As they are blunt nosed, instead of cutting the waves, planing hulls smack them, sending great wedges of water rolling over the cuddy which not uncommonly pushes the front windscreen out of its rubber trim. The implications of this are terrible if a lot of electronic equipment is carried up front. Most of our boats have either riveted shatter proof screens, or external swell guards. Struggling through the surf can be a prolonged task, as these boats rarely come fitted out for rowing. Brian and I have both fitted rowlocks. Many of our friends use paddles Red Indian style, which is all right for getting out, but what if you break down miles off? Finally, there is a tendency for cathedral hulls to wallow and slap noisily at anchor.

Could any list of good points ever hope to offset such criticism? Well, being flat bottomed, they are for the most part very wide and stable to walk about in, with the bonus of having parallel uniform beam. The room inside a 14 foot planer compared with a 16 foot traditional hull is very similar. The additional free-board (height above the water line) built into most planing designs really gives that big boat feeling of security while maintaining a manageable size. Being totally GRP moulded, save for a quick hose down and periodical keel inspection, little regular mainenance is necessary. These are shallow drafted boats (very little below the water line), well capable of coming off the trailer in water of ankle depth. That problem of getting the thing into water deep enough to run the engine can be beaten by fixing a diving ladder to the transom. Simply push the boat out and climb aboard. Once running, the turn of speed can be incredible. At times there may be a tendency to over shoot inshore marks on account of the short steaming times involved. Master this, and you have cracked it; not that all marks lie close to shore. If they did, speed would offer no advantage.

Above all else, never choose a boat purely on appearances. That it must be seen to be in good condition when buying second hand goes without saying, but why buy a sleek, smart looking flier to fish marks lying within half a mile of a steep shingle shore? Likewise, what good is a new displacement boat for fishing out of a harbour overlooking fishing grounds many miles from shore? Match all your requirements in terms of size, weight, proposed marks and expected sea conditions to the final choice, and try wherever possible to avoid too much wood. As one who has had to look after more wood than average, I should know what I'm talking about. As for wooden clinker boats, I would not entertain one for beach launching and trailing. They are strong, seaworthy and excellent riders, travelling more deeply in the water as opposed to bobbing about like GRP boats tend to do.

But all that maintenance......... still, some maintenance will be required whatever the construction. Ignorance and neglect of this fact will lead to rapid deterioration of any current boat building material.

Maintenance

Even GRP will age. To help satisfy the need for a quick turnover, some boat builders working in moulded GRP seem not to be bothered about certain time-honoured techniques in ensuring a good 'lay down'. Outwardly, the moulding will look no different. The first layer into a mould is a good thick coat of gel, supposedly followed by a covering of fine tissue, the light weight matting, then the really heavy stuff. If you are lucky, expensive woven matting will also have been used in all the crucial spots like keels and corners. This carries on until the desired weight of lay down is achieved; that is the theory behind GRP hull construction. Some look perilously wafer thin in places, and most have their heavy matting put straight on top of the gel once it starts to go off. As heavy matting cannot be worked properly into tight corners, invariably, air pockets beneath the gel occur. On even slight impact, these obviously cave in. Apart from looking a mess, gel damage can have serious consequences too. In short, layers of unsealed resin-layed matting are not on their own watertight. To seal a boat properly requires gel on the outside, a lack of which can lead to osmosis. In this instance, it is absorbtion of water into the body of the GRP wall, ultimately leading to deterioration and separation of the fibre layers. To define the term correctly, osmosis is the passing of liquids, but not dissolved solids, through a semi-permeable membrane. Never allow water too much time in contact with unprotected GRP matting.

Fibre glass resin, despite its overpowering smell and insistence in 'going off' either too quickly, or seemingly not at all, should present few problems if used in small amounts for alterations, or to effect minor repairs. For internal jobs like covering wooden hull support ribs, fitting a water tight bulkhead, or glassing in bouyancy tanks, ensure the entire surface to be treated is dry, grease and paint free. Wipe it with a rag soaked in acetone to both clean and soften the existing GRP. Then mix just a little resin with a drop of hardener in a clean tin can, using it to dab a few holding bits of mat into position. After this has set, cut larger pieces and mix more resin. Hardener can be added at around half a teaspoon to the pint, or as instructed by the supplier. Be sure the matting is well soaked, although not to the point when it becomes over resin-rich and large scale runs start to appear. Dab in the resin with a paint brush, keeping the brush in a jar of acetone between jobs. Most additional structures require at least two fixing layers of mat. At all times keep the job dry. Resin goes off much quicker in warm weather. It may well remain tacky for several days, despite being firm and solid. In time it will become what the experts term 'cured' — to you or I, dry to the touch.

Gel repairs are very much more straightforward. When buying resin or gel, colouring compound is available for addition during the hardener mixing stage. Gel is to all intents and purposes, thick jellified resin, except that it 'goes off' better when air is excluded. After mixing the required amounts, blob some into the hole or chip, and cover with a layer of wide Sellotape. Done carefully, the tape will ensure the new gel blends perfectly and smoothly with the old. If not, rub it down with a piece of fine grade wet or dry rubbing down paper. Take note though, that this can leave the area looking rather dull. On a keel, it doesn't matter much, but on the cuddy, for example, it could look an awful mess. Wood too can be treated these days with relative ease. Where previously hours of laborious preparation were required to re-do varnish, with today's modern applications, wood treatment can now be applied in a matter of minutes as and when required. Of course, there is a drawback. Before this new treatment can be applied, all the old varnish must first be removed. Where a new boat is being ordered with wood on it, ask the builder to leave it un-treated. It is to his advantage as well as yours. This revolutionary application is a Scandinavian saturation treatment called Deksolje. I have been using it for years. Initially, it takes around thirty coats, one immediately on top of the last while still wet. As it goes on like water, covering even large areas is easy. Eventually, the wood can soak up no more, leaving that remaining on top to dry to a pleasing satin finish. Deksolje also manufacture a gloss covering. As the saturation covering either wears or ages, a quick lick restores it in minutes. Sandpaper and scrapers are a thing of the past. I even treat my oars and landing net handle.

Brand new boats come equipped to varying degrees, depending of course on individual manufacturers, but I have yet to see one I would consider as up to scratch for regular use. They invariably fall well short of the angler's needs. Things to be checking for include oars, rowlocks, fairleads, cleats and decking boards. Galvanised keel bands fitted as standard are a real rarity. Stainless transom plates to prevent engine clamp damage are always a home job. Does it have a bilge plug? A bulkhead up front for either the anchor or loose clothing would be handy. A new boat may well be fit for the odd trip in between bouts of bringing it up to scratch. To think that because it is new it is perfect, is pure folly. Fitting out, though time consuming, is quite cheap. Building up a proper ancillary kit is far from that. If you cannot afford the many extras, such as anchors, ropes, compass, life jackets, flares and the rest as well as the cost of the boat you should give up the idea completely. The necessities may be expensive but being lost at sea through thrift is a bigger price to pay. Nobody ever actually wants to use safety equipment, but carrying it is an absolute must.

Essential Ancillary Equipment

Compass — it matters little which end of the price range you look to, so long as you have one available at all times, can rely on it, and above all know how to use the thing, a fact discussed in navigation a little later on. As soon as the anchor bites hold, take a reading for a straight line course back to your launching point, then if fog descends, panic does not come down with it. Above all, recognise the fact that your compass knows its way home better than you think you do. I know at times mistrust can set in, particularly after a long time steaming with still no glimpse of land. It would be suicidal at that point to head off on a different 'I'm certain it's this way' course. If you are likely to mistrust your compass, or like me, feel happier with a bit of additional assurance, as well as fitting a good boat version, carry a small Silva orienteering compass in your pocket to double check. They are cheap and extremely reliable, providing as in the case of all magnetic compasses, they are used well away from steel or electrical gadgetry. Look for the 'cleanest' spot on board — probably the centre of the fishing well, then compare your hand reading with that of the fixed compass situated perhaps on the cuddy roof, or screwed to a set. A fixed compass can be checked and adjusted by a qualified setter to compensate for faulty readings brought about by surrounding metals and equipment. Finally, a word for fast boat enthusiasts. Ask for a compass designed and dampened for use at speed; otherwise the rose will be floating and bobbling all over the place under power.

Flares — should you get into difficulties, of primary concern is letting other people know about it. With the exception of a VHF radio, nothing does this better than a flare, but not just any old flare. Different signals can mean different things. Here are the coastguard recommendations........

Small boats up to 7 miles out — 4 two star red signals, 4 red hand flares and 2 orange smoke flares.

Small boats over 7 miles out — 4 red parachute rockets, 4 red hand flares and 2 buoyant orange smoke signals.

In the areas frequented by commercial shipping, the carrying of 4 white smoke flares is advisable for use should a collision look imminent, and we further recommend the carrying of a rocket, even for trips of under 3 miles. Having flares is one thing, knowing how to use them is something else, and the wrong time to be getting first hand experience is when bobbing around neck deep in a cold lumpy sea. Flares come with a recommended replacement date stamped on them. It might not be a bad idea for everyone to try letting off at least one in date, or just out dated flare somewhere carefully chosen so as not to create alarm. As old outdated flares quickly become unstable and unpredictable, do not play with them. Contact the coastguard to arrange disposal.

Life jackets — ignorance is rife on this subject. Ask most people if they carry life jackets and they usually answer "Yes", and genuinely believe they are, though in many cases they are not. The fact is, most small boat anglers carry buoyancy aids, which are far from the same thing. The term buoyancy aid is self explanatory, as is the term life jacket. A buoyancy aid will help if you can help yourself. Life jackets on the other hand support the head and face upwards, even when the wearer is unconscious. Few people, and I am as guilty as the rest, bother to wear a life jacket at all times. Recognising this fact, while hardly condoning it, at least have the thing to hand at all times. Orally inflated jackets of the type carrying an emergency CO_2 cylinder inside are the easiest of all to wear constantly. On the outside of waterproofs, they are exposed to flying hooks. Underneath the top layer they are no problem at all. So flat are they in fact, even with the recommended bit of air already inside, it is hard to tell it is there. Buoyancy aids on the other hand are cumbersome, and as they make a comfortable seat cushion, this then is how many end up, which is about all they are fit for anyway. Charter boats are required to carry life jackets by law in order to comply with the Department of Trade (DOT) regulations. Jackets with DOT approval are not the same as those on sale in boating supply shops, which are up to the British Standard (BS) specification, and far from the same thing. Kapok stuffed life jackets often get DOT approval, and incidentally, though quite bulky, will properly support an unconscious person, and at a fraction of the cost of the alternative buoyancy aids included. Whistle — small boats are required by law to carry some means of giving out a sound signal at sea. A whistle is an acceptable means, though a canister foghorn could also be carried. Rather than cut out the whistle in favour of a foghorn, put it in your fishing jacket pocket, or attach it to a life jacket. That way, should you end up separated from your boat in fog, it could prove a life saver in drawing attention to your position.

Had the planing boat in the background been fitted with rowlocks, laborious paddling would not have been necessary.

Oars — in dealing with planing boats earlier, it was pointed out that most have no facility for rowing. Even some displacement boats when fitted with rowlocks, still come without oars. On a planing boat, have rowlocks fitted, and in both cases, be sure to carry oars suited to the job. Oars are useful in propelling a boat through the surf into water deep enough to start the engine running. More importantly, they can, no matter how much the struggle, be the lifeline in getting you back inshore should the engine fail. Be sure and buy the correct length for the boat. When sitting in a central rowing position, both oar blades should be well into the water at a comfortable angle. Sizes and needs vary greatly, so take advice, as a good pair will not come cheap. As a guide, our 14 foot planing boats take eight footers, while those aboard my 16 footer with its broad beam are nines. A word too about rowlocks. Avoid all but good strong galvanised versions. Various plastics are all right for playing about, but when you put your back into the rowing, the oars repeatedly spring out.

Anchor — this is your only means of applying the brakes or parking at sea, a necessity outside the safety arena for many aspects of bottom fishing. If the engine packs up, staying put while trying to summon assistance is crucial. An obvious question here would be to ask how long an anchor rope should be. How long indeed? It does of course depend on the depth of water beneath the hull. A recommended figure is at least three times the depth. Experience has shown this to be inadequate on all but the calmest of days. Swell playing games with the tension of the rope may frequently dislodge the hold. Even more rope and chain is not always the answer, though undoubtedly it must help. So my answer to the question is, to make it as long as you can. The length can always be checked and tied off in shallow water. Too much rope, like too much chain, would be impossible. At least 10 to 12 feet of good galvanised chain will be required to give the anchor a proper bite. What you can end up with is the wrong anchor for the job.

Anchors should be matched to seabed conditions. Here again, seek and take advice from other local anglers. I often get asked which is the best all round compromise anchor. The truth of the matter is, as with boats, the perfect all rounder has not, and will not be designed. This said, I suppose the Bruce shows the greatest range of versatility. Like the jointed plough, it is basically a sand anchor. Another good design, particularly over heavier ground and amongst stones, is the old faithful fisherman's anchor like the one tattooed on Popeye's arm. For heavy rock, a light grapnel may work best. There are a number of shapes as well as sizes to choose from. For both my boats I carry a 2 kg Bruce and a 10 pound plough. Even for smaller boats I wouldn't go any lighter. Far better to be too heavy than too light.

You will notice on the main stem of most anchors, a hole at both ends. That furthest from the point is its normal chain shackle hole, offering a simple direct pull when holding over clean ground. In areas where there is a possibility of its going to ground and staying stuck, fix the shackle in the other hold, taking the chain up along the main stem, lashing it in what will

Phil Williams with the British record spotted ray, taken over patchy ground in Loch Ryan. Note the fisherman's anchor suited to this type of seabed.

then appear a normal position, using a few wraps of orange corlene string through the upper hole. It will then work in a conventional manner, until it gets stuck. Constant pressure should snap the corlene threads, causing the anchor to invert and free itself. Getting the balance of corlene threads is, I'm afraid, a trial and error job.

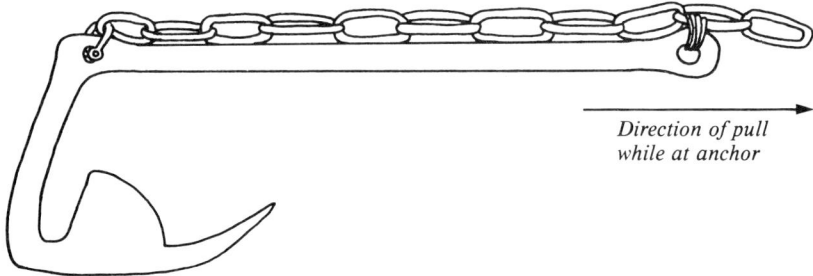

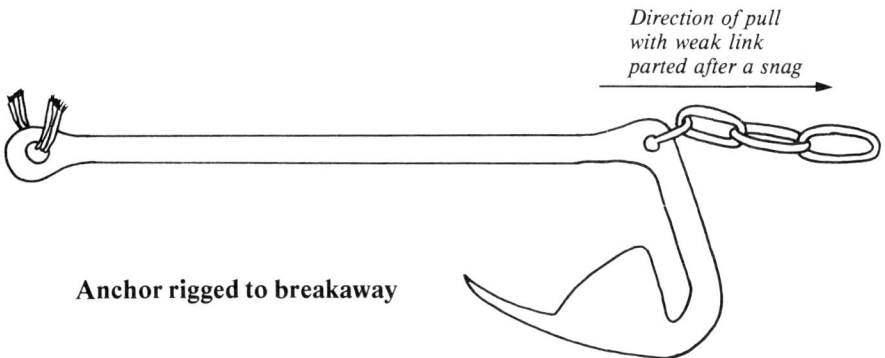

Direction of pull while at anchor

Direction of pull with weak link parted after a snag

Anchor rigged to breakaway

Take the boat a little way uptide of your mark, lowering the anchor down until it impacts with the sea bed. Now you can either wait to be taken the rope's length on the tide, or carefully reverse away under power. Never under any circumstance pitch the whole rope overboard and sit back until the tide stretches it tight. One chap up our way did that in a heavy sea, the result being a coil snagged around his propeller bringing him to rest stern into the swell. Within minutes, the boat was swamped and sank. Only a quick mayday on the VHF radio saved him, for despite having sailed out and anchored up in company, nobody saw him go down.

Torch — essential with or without fixed lighting, and should be carried both day and night. Apart from the obvious advantage of assisting the replacement of a blown fuse in the dark, or directing the net to a fish lost in a shadow area close into the boat, consider the fact that although you may only intend fishing by day, due to engine failure, you could still be out there after dark. A useful signalling device as well as a tool.

Baler — some means of removing excessive amounts of water caused either by swamping at the launch, or a heavy rainfall, is vital. It could be anything from a small bait bucket to a flask top. I think if it required a bucket I would be very concerned. In the main, makeshift balers are round, and as such cannot get into tight corners or remove shallowish water from flat surfaces. What I did was cut an oblong half gallon orange cordial container along its diagonals, retaining the half with the handle, giving a perfect baler well able to scoop up every last drop.

Fish box — if you manage to find a few fish, they could well turn out to be as much a danger as they are a source of enjoyment if not kept properly. At any time, dead fish, or the slime they leave is hazardous under foot. Even if you up-end yourself and land inside the boat cushioned by the culprit it still hurts. So keep all fish tidily contained up front out of harm's way. Besides being good sense, it means less mess to clean up later.

Tool kit — major engine repairs are not only nigh on impossible, but highly impracticable at sea. Minor problems on the other hand though they may only take a few minutes to remedy given all the necessaries, can still mean a long row back to the beach but not necessarily so if a small emergency repair kit is put together. Nothing elaborate — a plug spanner, spare plugs, emery paper, feeler guage, tin of grease, little oil can, WD40, some PVC tape and small jubilee clips for fuel line repairs, pull cord or piece of light rope, small screwdriver, pliers, spare throttle cable and a few useful spanners will more than suffice. However makeshift or temporary, getting back to shore under power is the prime objective. A more lasting repair can be carried out later on at home, but how does one go about carrying and remembering not only the listed tools, but all the other necessary items? In an open boat, the last thing anybody wants is little piles of delicate, 'not-to-be-got-wet' bits lying all around the place. What I use is a large plastic bucket with a press on watertight lid to house the lot. Ever dry and always ready, nothing gets left behind. The tub can even double up as a seat, or in a real emergency, when emptied, as a buoyancy aid.

Optional ancillary equipment

Spare bilge plug — small, yet potentially vital. Plugs are easily lost or damaged. It seems such a waste to let the cost and enjoyment of an entire outing hinge on a small bit of cheap plastic. Pop a spare one into the tool tub.

Spare anchor — the need to prevent being blown out to sea in the event of engine failure has already been covered, but what if you lose an anchor? It is funny how problems often compound themselves. Make sure a second anchor is both up to any job it might be called upon to do, and well equipped with rope and chain.

Lazy line — bringing a boat to anchor, even with a cuddy fitted, is straight forward enough. When re-visiting marks on a regular basis, rope length becomes something of a constant. As such it can all be paid out, providing the end is permanently fixed up front. That way, the boat lies comfortably nose into the tide. With cuddied boats, problems only start to arise when the time for hauling back comes around. If there is a hatch, all well and good.

Where there is no such access, gingerly crawling along the walkway in a pitching sea is dangerous to say the least. Instead, we use what we call a 'lazy line'. This is nothing more than a length of rope with a metal eye fixed to one end, through which the main anchor rope has been passed before it was tied into place. By pulling on this line, the anchor rope is brought around to the side where it can be reached and hauled in safely. Tie the loose end of the line to a 'U' bolt or similar fastening in case it should vanish over the side, but never under any circumstances tie an anchor rope to a side position because you can not get up front. Anchoring broadside on to a running sea is dangerous, and could result in a swamping.

Fog horn — as already stated, all boats are required by law to carry some means of giving a sound signal. A small canister fog horn serves not only this purpose, but gives often needed re-assurance when at anchor in fog, particularly if you can hear the low pitched thudding of an approaching diesel engine. I know just how it feels to have this happen; a few quick blasts saved the day. They are not expensive, but be sure and shake the canister well before squeezing the fire button. If you don't, the horn gives a weak chesty cough, followed by a puff of white powder.

Cutting board — though far removed from actual safety equipment, to me, a cutting board for bait falls into the category of being absolutely essential. Slicing up mackerel in a boat does not do either varnish or gel coat a great deal of good. It also leaves a horrible gutsy mess sure to be sat on by someone.

Fire extinguisher — two types of fire hazard face the dinghy angler. The main threat really comes from combustible fuels such as petrol leaking from a hose, or paraffin from an upended Tilley lamp. The other cause is wiring faults. As so little in the way of complex wiring is necessary, the latter presents little, if any real threat. Adequately fused circuits will be safeguard enough. Fuel fires are another thing. Fuel line couplings wear and slacken with age. One carelessly dropped cigarette butt could 'warm things up' no end. The carrying of a small fire extinguisher is well recommended. It need contain no more than 1.5 kg of dry powder, suited to either of the fires discussed.

First aid kit — in dire emergency, there is not a lot you can expect to do in case of an accident out at sea, except make full steam for shore, using a VHF radio if carried to arrange assistance standing by. Most fishing accidents are pretty minor. Just the odd filleting knife slit, mis-placed hook, or chewed up fingers if you are lucky enough to catch a tope. Basically, these kind of injuries are best cared for with a tube of antiseptic cream, some plasters and the odd bandage or two. More serious bleeding may call for an improvised tourniquet using bandages twisted tight with a screwdriver or disgorger. And bits from the home medicine chest, or a specially put together kit will do well. Slip in a card of sea sick pills as well.

Bilge pump — an insurance measure essential on some styles of boat. My planing boat has an inner skin created by a false floor and buoyancy tanks. If

A good bilge pump can be very useful even in a small boat.

I were to hit a floating object at speed, holing the hull below the water line, I could be in all sorts of trouble. Many people remove their tank tops, using the space inside as lockers. Either way, water seeping into the cavity is going to prove a problem. If it fills a sealed space, while the boat cannot sink, it can't really be motored either due to its lying very low in the water. A friend of mine tells this story from a personal experience, having motored out to anchor with the bilge plugs still in his pocket. Without the tank tops, seeping water would eventually gush through the holes filling up the boat. Water lying inside the fishing well can be baled, but not that trapped between the two floor layers, and as fast as the excesses are baled, more bubbles through to replace it. Only a bilge pump can hope to cope. I cut a hole into the front of my buoyancy tank, threaded in a length of hose and jubilee clipped it to a short length of stainless tube brazed through a hole in a piece of flat plate. When fibre-glassed into position, re-sealing the tank, the short stub of tube still showing was hosed up to the pump situated and screwed to a piece of wood glassed onto the side of the boat. With this, clearing water from the cavity is a formality. A variety of pumps can be bought, including efficient little electric versions with a lower price mark-up than hand operated pumps. I still prefer a good quality British hand pump. Knowing my luck, the first time I take on water, the electric pump will fail.

Echo sounder — most modern sounders have built into them an automatic fail safe. In short, to avert accidents, when the battery starts to run down, the reading will be less than actual. This is not essential, but a useful device at times when fishing over shallow lying rocks, or navigating a narrow channel. We use ours purely and simply as an aid to fishing. Both are of simple lit dial type. I can see no justification whatsoever for a big print-out on a majority of dinghies. Forget ideas of picking up shoals of fish or identifying different sea beds. This is one maker's claim I feel positively unable to help bear out. Mine is used for picking out narrow gullies up which I think cod move in search of food deposited by the tide. It is not so much the using that caused problems, but the knowing of how to fit it that puts a lot of people off.

The part used to send out and catch the bounced signal — the transducer, needs to be fitted in an area of the floor (never an inner skin, but the actual hull) away from water turbulence, and in a position guaranteed to be covering water at the time each reading is being taken. There is little point in installing the thing way up front in a fast boat clogging along at full bore. Providing the GRP laydown does not exceed ¾ of an inch, and that it is not placed over a wooden side runner or galvanised band, all should be well. Transducers are capable of firing their signal through the hull without any need for drilling a hole. A kit can be bought containing a length of tube for fixing to the hull, and a bottle of caster oil. Actually, I made my own by building layers of fibre glass around a specially machined and polished piece of steel bar. This I later angle-cut at the bottom to suit the hull, giving the tube a vertical standing when glassed into position. A small amount of mixed resin poured into the base seals it fully. That the transducer stands perfectly vertical is imperative to ensure a good direct signal. Any gap and resultant air space caused by the angle is filled with caster oil. The latter was chosen because of its relatively low freezing point.

Radio — an expensive luxury perhaps, but should I get into difficulties, I want to know that everybody else knows. After a while, VHF becomes a necessity; even a way of life. Brian and I can shoot off in different directions comparing results as the fishing develops. Or it could well be that I might want to stay out longer than planned, so a call to one of the others going ashore ensures a telephone call home to put the wife's mind at rest. At night, I always radio the coastguard, getting him to chalk up the boat name, number of persons on board, area being fished and ETA back on shore on his blackboard. This covers us in case of an emergency. You can incidentally do this by telephone. Just don't forget to tell him you have arrived back safe and well afterwards. I do not think the rescue services would take too kindly to looking for you all night while you're tucked up in bed.

My first radio was a pocket size, one watt output, six channel handset, which I wired to a big cuddy top aerial to improve transmission. I have since switched to a larger set. Not that there was anything wrong with the other; just a natural progression. Having bought a boat carrying a 12 volt supply, it seemed only natural to want a higher powered transmission output. Into the bargain I got many more channels, though these I could just as easily have done without. All sets come with channels 16, the emergency and call up channel, and 6, which is designated intership, fitted as standard. There is

Hand set with integral battery suited for small open boats, and larger externally fed set for use where battery weight is no problem.

also a need for channel 67, which is the small boat safety channel. Ship to ship channels vary in their local patronage, so check with other radio buffs for the right ones to have put in. Operating the set is remarkably straight forward. Perhaps choosing a good set and suitable aerial will require a little unbiased advice, which, along with a one day course leading to a Home Office approved marine band VHF limited user's licence, can be had from your nearest nautical college. Failing this, contact the Home Office, Waterloo Bridge House, Waterloo Road, London SE1 8UA. Stick with an approved international marine band VHF, leaving CB sets for the breakers back on shore.

As power in small boats is fed from a 12 volt D.C. supply such as a car battery, then boat wiring can be considered as auto wiring, but on a very much simpler scale. It all boils down to satisfying personal needs along with those of the law. By bringing a twin, or two single 44s guage cable as a main feed from the battery to a central distribution box in a suitable position such as the cuddy, each unit can then be fed with its own simple individual circuit. Fused distribution boards can either be improvised or bought specially, the two musts being that sufficient room be available in the terminal block, and that it is damp sealed with a rubber rim or smear of silicone grease. Dampness is a fact of life with boats. In the winter, accumulated condensation freezes overnight, then thaws the following day, leaving water running everywhere. Let every connection, be it an auto snap, push on

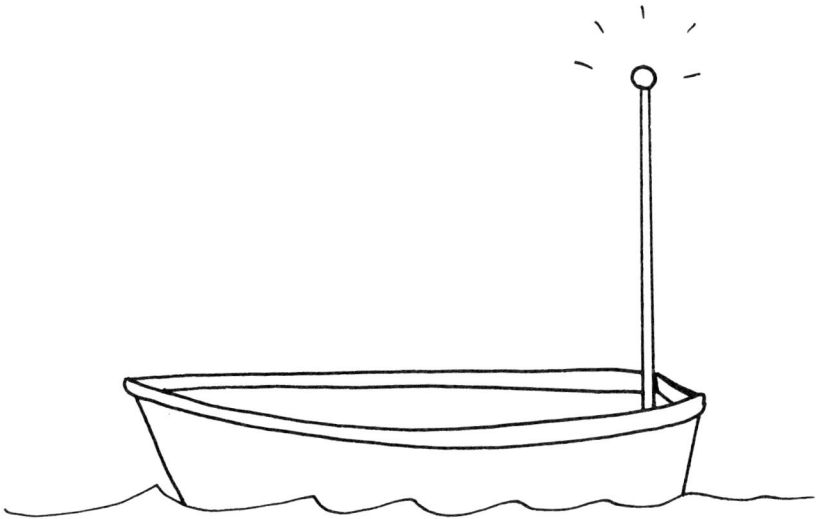

Legal lighting requirement for an open boat at night – one uplifted all round white light.

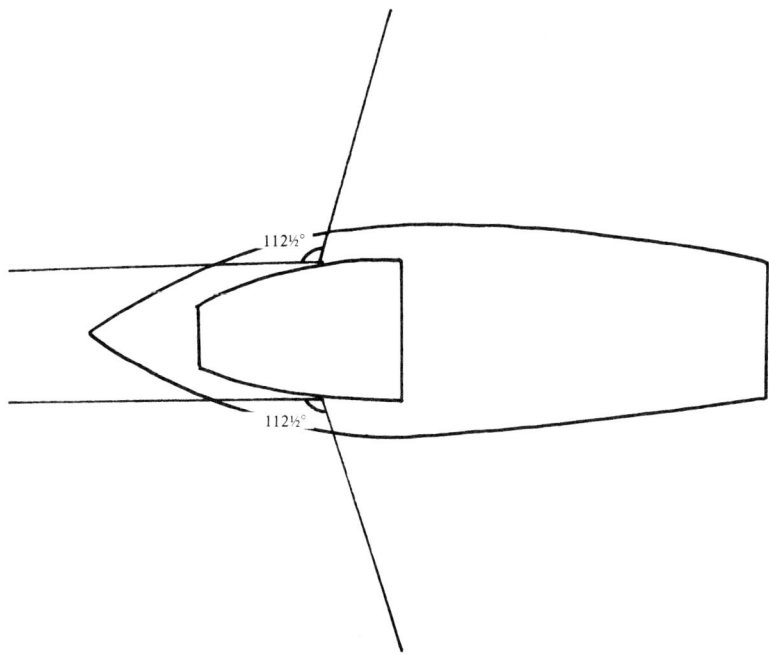

112½°

112½°

Positioning of navigation lights.

terminal, or screwed block, even the battery lugs and their connections, have a good smear of Vaseline or silicone grease to prevent corrosion attacking the joint. Lighting, and the range of instruments available, differs greatly. Even so, each relies on a positive feed and negative return, unlike car wiring where one lug of the battery is shorted to the car chassis, with the negative wire from each unit also bolted to the frame, allowing electricity returning to the battery to do so via the car body in order to save on wire. With wood and GRP this is obviously out of the question; not that an earth return is recommended anyway out at sea. To switch a unit, simply break into the positive wire, putting each cut end to either terminal of your switch.

Before pressing on with individual circuitry, here are the lighting regulations. Boats of less than 7 metres, or travelling at less than 7 knots must show an all round white light, and port (red) and starboard (green) navigation lights are to be fitted whenever practicable. Just a brief word here about the choice of lights. Coloured navigation lights must conform to precise angles. Buying approved makes usually ensures these are built in automatically. An all round white light must be shown at anchor and like all other lights must be visible for a range of at least 2 miles, so it's both sets for a boat with a cuddy, and just the white light for an open boat. My 360 degree light came fitted to a raised tubular stand with a wide base for bolting to the roof. Height obviously increases the range of visibility, particularly at sea where pitching and rolling can partially obscure a very low placed light. For open boats, their version usually comes on a tall stand fitted to the stern.

Boats exceeding 7 metres and/or travelling at speeds in excess of 7 knots, were until recently, required to display a forward pointing 225 degree white light and a stern facing 135 degree white light. Port and starboard navigation lights completed the steaming requirements, with a 360 degree white light for use at anchor. Now, boats of under 12 metres can show a 360 degree white light in lieu of the split steaming lights, providing they show port and starboard navigation lights at a point at least one metre lower. Lighting legislation is often contradictory, dependent upon source, and in any case, is prone to regular change. For all shipping legislation, consult Reeds Nautical Almanac, in this case International regulations for preventing collisions at sea 1972 (amended 1983).

When approaching another vessel head on, boats should pass port to port, which is red to red, exactly the opposite of cars on the road. However, as well as having lights to be seen, there are lights for seeing with. For fishing after dark, the two most popular seeing lights are either a car reversing lamp of up to 21 watts, fitted mid cuddy looking down into the fishing well, or a paraffin pressure lamp. Tillies give off more than adequate light, not to mention heat. Positioned carefully, they should present no problems. Certainly, I have yet to hear of one going up in flames out at sea. Light the thing back on shore, and if it is so rough that it falls over, what are you doing out after dark in the first place? And do not forget to take along a little jar of methylated spirits.

The length of a distribution box feed and its neat concealed run from the battery, depends on the style of boat and positioning of the battery. Planing boats with electric ignition need their battery at the back, giving the shortest starter leads possible to minimise voltage drop. Shoved under the splash well, it is advisable to protect the battery from the elements. Even up front, a purpose built strap down box is worth its money in stopping acid splashing all over the place. Alternatively, buy a fully sealed battery. Whatever its position, when running cables through small sharp holes, use a rubber grommet to prevent the insulation chaffing. Failing a grommet, a blob of silicone rubber compound of the type used to make glass-to-glass fish tanks is ideal. It sets like solid transparent rubber, and is equally useful for sealing windows, or smearing under fittings to be clamped tightly into position, such as lights, handrails, bilge pump housings and the like. Inside the distribution box, after completing all the connections, a good application of Vaseline or silicone grease is strongly recommended, the latter particularly if it can be obtained in spray form. With lighting, it doesn't matter which wire goes to which terminal; only with instruments must the positive feed match the positive input connection.

Navigation lights — two lengths of single core, or one length of twin core 14s gauge cable with a cartridge loading in line 5 amp fuse placed in the positive wire. Should an on/off switch be required, this too is broken into the positive wire as shown in the circuit diagram, which is the case with all circuits. Navigation lights involve the use of two light units working together. For all single light units, two lengths of single core, or a single length of twin core 14s guage cable is ample, with a 2 amp in line fuse fitted to the positive wire which should also carry the switch if required, fitted in a

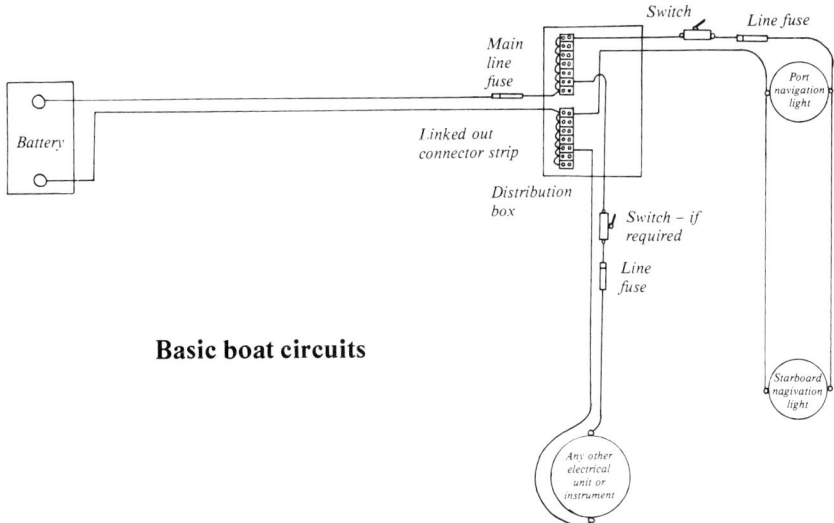

Basic boat circuits

convenient position along the positive wire's length, preferably inside the cuddy.

Radio — two lengths of single core, or one length of twin core 14s guage cable with an in line fuse carrier fitted to both wires. This allows total disconnection of the radio for removal. Actual fuse sizes vary with radio output. For 1 to 10 watts use a 3 amp fuse. A 25 watt output set requires a 5 amp fuse.

Echo sounders, compass lights and the rest can be fed with lengths of 14s guage cable and fused at around 3 amps. The use of individual in line fuses to protect each unit is not totally necessary, but is advisable in light of the cost of some instruments, as is the addition of another in line fuse fitted to the main positive feed from the battery. The strength of this particular fuse will depend on the total amperage taken in the unlikely event of everything electrical on board being in use simultaneously. To arrive at this value, simply add all the other fuse strengths together. And be sure to carry a selection of spares tucked inside the box. In an emergency, any of the higher rated fuses can be temporarily used to replace a lower rated one that has blown. Here the problem is in knowing why it has blown. Has the circuit developed a fault? More often than not, fuses blow out of fatigue or old age. Trying a stronger replacement is up to you. But if it is an emergency ....
Electronic aids and on board lighting, even in a dinghy, make for a more comfortable and secure life, but the more you tag on, the greater the drain on the battery. Life can become pretty miserable at sea when the power fails. Always the first thing to suffer is electronic ignition, followed closely by radio transmission, though not reception, which takes hardly any current at all. Batteries such as on small boats not in constant use, won't have the life span of a similar battery carried on a regularly used car. It is a case of an overnight spell on the charger before every trip. Electronic ignition and plenty of chattering on full powered transmission are the two biggest drains. A charge could well last a couple of trips, depending of course on the job it is being asked to perform. One other point, batteries gradually lose their charge when left for long periods such as during in prolonged winter gales.

Lighting leads us nicely into the subject of night fishing. After dark, some species of fish lose all their daylight inhibitions, while others prefer nocturnal feeding simply as a matter of course. Either way, the fact that fish become very much more active close to shore cannot be disputed, which is great news for small boaters in that we need not stray quite so far from dry land in order to get at them. I look upon night fishing as something of a bonus. Only rarely I do it in preference to day time fishing. It has often been said that night fishing is best left to the experienced. Certainly it is not the kind of pursuit to be undertaken alone; neither is it advisable for one boat to venture out alone. But if, you do put to sea on your own, fix a lanyard to your belt. That way, should you fall overboard, at least you can get back to the boat. The question is, how does a person gain experience without ever giving it a try? When all persons on board can perform whatever job they have been delegated without question, it is time to be giving night fishing a go. It is for the most part safer than daylight fishing in that having every single day from which to choose, you will only venture out when sea conditions are absolutely perfect. Weekend anglers, faced with another five days of nothing in front of them, are more likely to take chances than a crew willing to try again tomorrow, and tomorrow and so on. But I don't think you ever really get used to being out in the dark. Sailing out into total darkness is an experience all of its own. Other boats appear like ghosts in a dream. Swells always look twice as big as the faint moonlight glints on their slopes. This is one occasion when the constant wearing of life jackets is a must. Eyes quickly become accustomed to conditions, whether there is good back lighting or not. It pays to wrap rod tips with a few inches of reflective tape. Hooking and playing out a fish to the net is a fantastic feeling. What sticks in my mind most of all are big staring eyes piercing coldly through me from the base of the yellow torch beam.

What individuals choose to put on the back of boats as a source of power is entirely their own affair. We have already discussed matching engine capacity to hull design but it is equally important to match engine shaft length to transom depth. As you will have gathered, not all engines are of like standard. Most bigger boats take long shaft engines. By fitting a standard, all you end up with is plenty of gurgle and spray for very little movement. With the water intake unable to suck up sufficient coolant, in no time at all the engine will be ruined. Find out exactly which shaft length your particular boat requires before parting with the cash. Perhaps the most important thing to know about outboard engines, is how to treat them with respect. Regular servicing, flushing and cleaning are a must. Routine preventative maintenance should come after every trip. Just a few minutes spent getting rid of the salt from the cooling system and casing is both simple and vital. Small, unbolted engines should be removed and put to drain on the pavement while the rest of the boat is readied for home. We carry ours in the car boot. Others prefer to lash theirs down inside the boat on an old piece of carpet. Back home it is clamped to a wooden frame, then run in a large tub of freshwater. Pump the carburettor full to start it running, disconnecting the fuel line immediately leaving the engine to run both in and out of gear until the fuel gives out. Be sure though that the cooling system is circulating water through. Now a quick wipe down, a blast of WD40 under the cowl, and back onto the wooden support frame in the garage until next trip. Large, permanently fixed engines have adapters allowing direct hose flushing straight from the tap. Most engine problems come as a direct result of neglect. Internal salt accumulation is just one reason. Not regularly checking spark plugs, simple as it may sound, is another. Plugs soon become too gummed up to fire properly, particularly when insufficient attention is paid to two stroke fuel oil mix. Follow the manufacturer's instructions to the letter, and buy in proper marine two stroke mix from a chandler, not just any old oil from the nearest filling station.

Permanently fixed engines need to comply with the law when in transit on the road. Because when tilted, the propeller protrudes further than the lighting board, it presents a hazard to other road users. A reflective bag must be fitted, making other road users aware of the extent of the protrusion. Only with a trailer board specially bracketed beyond the propeller can the bag be dispensed with.

Now two final thoughts as engines are expensive commodities: when road trailing with the thing in position and on tilt, wedge a strip of wood under the tilt mechanism to prevent either its jolting, or breaking free should you hit a bad bump. And when travelling at sea, all small clamped engines should have the secondary security of a lanyard in case they work free of the transom. Believe it or not, this does happen. Far better to have the engine swamped but retrieved, rather then see it sink forever. Immediate treatment of an immersed engine by a recognised outboard dealer could possible avert a total write off.

Road Trailers

Road trailers are not so much chosen, as matched to specific boats. Poor matching can lead to hull damage if a boat bounces up and down loosely on its side supports. Some measure of choice is available with things like roller style, galvanising and the option of a good winch, which really is an absolute necessity. If well treated and maintained there is no real reason why a trailer cannot last the life of the boat it carries. Constant immersion in salt water, if not counteracted, will take its toll with untreated steel. Protection can be achieved in two ways. Galvanising is the 'Rolls Royce' answer. This is a dipped coating of zinc plate. As it works inside all the hollow sections, life expectancy is obviously very high. Zinc plating can be applied to trailers of any age. By virtue of the fact that no sand blasting is required to depaint a new trailer, it then will be cheaper. The platers themselves then dip the metal into acid, and finally into the hot zinc bath. Removal of rollers, winch, suspension units and mudguards goes without saying. Cost of the whole operation can prove surprisingly less than a good paint job treatment from new. The problem with paint is getting it inside the hollow sections. By breaking down the trailer, if possible, paint can be poured down each of the inner flats in turn, collected at the other end to be sent through again. A few coats of good red oxide primer, followed by a gloss covering and whatever else is favoured, will, if touched in regularly before rust can spread, keep the steel in good order. During the annual 'dead period' around March to April, off come the hubs for a check, paraffin wash and re-grease. All the rollers and winch cable are checked, and a complete new coat of paint is given to the whole unit. Regular freshwater hosing at the same time as the boat and engines are flushed will minimise a lot of corrosion.

Like everything else using the road these days, boat trailers are governed by law. They must have mudguards and adequate lighting. In some instances, they may also require their own independent brakes. This only becomes necessary when the gross laden weight of a trailed unit exceeds half the gross kerb weight of its towing vehicle. But more often than not, it is faulty trailer lights that invite the attention of the law. Always, on plugging in a trailer unit, check each individual lighting function both individually, then collectively, before setting off. Should something be amiss, try the board on another car. If the fault persists, then the board is to blame. If not, start checking over the car. Far and away the single most common lighting fault is the mobile disco effect of everything flashing on and off at once. This is nothing worse than a bad earth, resulting in the other bulbs getting back feeds. In almost every case, the earth wire in the trailer plug will have pulled free. Another lighting fault is only having one tail light working on the board right from the moment the seven pin plug is fitted. This is the result of taking the tail light feed only one side of the car. Either take the car back to the electrician who wired it, or run a short length of 14s gauge cable from one bulb to that on the other side.

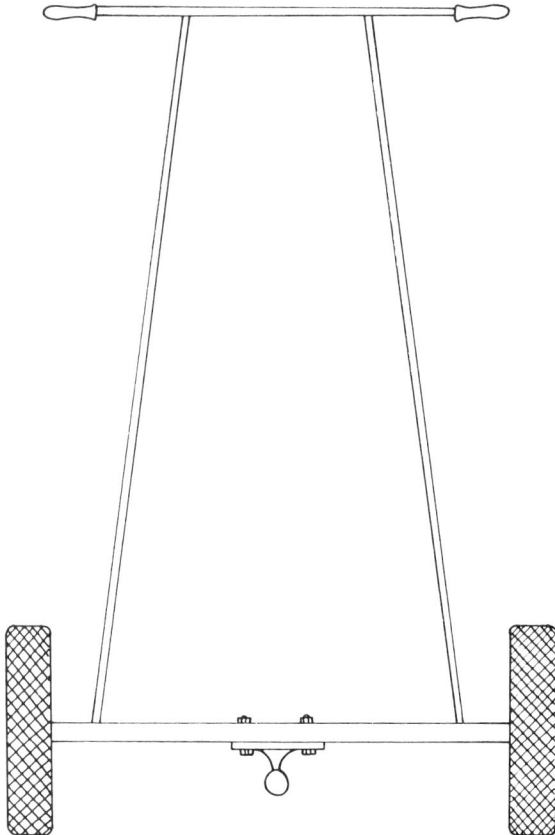

Beach launching trolley used to convert two wheeled trailer into four wheeled unit.

Once the routine of preparation and trailing is worked out, few problems should occur. Balancing the boat on the axle is important. With an adjustable axle, this is not difficult. Load inside the boat can have some bearing here. Too much nose weight pushing down on the car ball hitch will impair the steering. Make sure you carry the right gear for a puncture. Surely everyone carries a spare wheel, but is the car jack suited to lifting the trailer? If not, get one from a local scrapyard. Also, carry a spare boat strap or length of rope in case your other gets damaged. I have already made mention of the problems associated with boats bouncing about loosely. Digressing a little yet again, for beach trailing where there are no tractor facilities, we have devised a front launching trolley which is carried inside the boat. It is simply a piece of angle iron, not exceeding the boat's beam, to which is welded a suitable stub for a hub and wheel. A tubular handle is welded to its front. By means of a towball bolted mid point, the boat is hitched into position, creating a four wheeled unit. As no muscle power is required to keep the front end up, every effort can be applied to forward movement. By choosing hubs and wheels to match those of the trailer, inter-changability may help in case of a roadside breakdown. Where possible, choose the biggest wheels available, giving greater ground clearance for avoiding boulders, and a wider surface area over soft sand. Most people I know buy mini-hubs from the scrapyards. I recall once launching on the edge of dark, bumping into a chap I know who had just rowed ashore with a broken engine shaft. To make things worse, his wheels bogged down in the soft sand. Try as we might, they wouldn't budge. Nothing else for it but side to side shoving in the hope of freeing one side at a time. In the end we pushed the hubs out of the tyres!

Always regard your fishing rig not as money spent, but as an investment, treating it as such by seeing that it is properly insured. No matter what degree of insurance coverage the towing vehicle has, its trailer requires separate treatment. Many brokers deal with reputable specialists in maritime insurance, offering coverage for loss at sea, third party liability as personal protection from claims made by a swimmer or crew member, which might run into many thousands of pounds, and finally, on the road security. Risks are never higher than when road trailing to or from the coast. If somebody runs into you, all well and good, his insurers must cough up. In bad weather, accidents can take on a shared blame basis, or even be totally of your own making, in which case trying to save a little will result in the loss of the lot. Choose a well known company. Most insurers will try and wriggle out of every claim, so leave no loop-holes. Even tell your car insurers of your intention to trail a boat. Another form of insurance is that of letting the coastguard know of your intentions while out at sea. In an attempt to further help others to help you, make certain the boat has its name clearly displayed on the hull. Not only that, fix a name plate and home telephone number to the trailer so that the authorities can readily check things out if a trailer appears to be spending too much time parked up on the beach. Strangers do get worried, and in many cases, genuinely want to help. Whenever possible, boats from our club try to at least stay in pairs, if not small groups. That way, the moment a problem arises, others are around to offer help in certain knowledge that one day their turn will eventually come. Most small boaters would be loathe to see one of their own ranks in dire trouble. But beware, for there are strict rules governing salvage. When in trouble, I know, you are glad to accept any assistance going, but those providing it are entitled to ask for a fee. I know one chap who was charged £40 for a tow back by a charter boat called out specifically to help him. The fee was negotiated in advance of the deal being struck and the tow line going across. If in doubt, ask your would-be rescuer his intentions, and if necessary, strike up an amicable agreement, preferably in writing. Obviously, in difficult circumstances, the last thing you need is to start formulating a written contract. With this in mind, we have pre-prepared one for carrying ready in the wallet. Once completed, you hang onto it. This could be your only proof of having struck up an agreement in order to avert a full salvage claim, and always let the person doing the towing provide the rope. This way the tow is seen to be a voluntary gesture.

The following is the format such a contract could take.

In the event of completing this document, I agree to forgo any subsequent claim on salvage or other monies for rendering assistance as quoted below.

BOAT NEEDING ASSISTANCE.....................

BOAT GIVING ASSISTANCE ....

ASSISTANCE REQUIRED...........................

SUM AGREED.....................................

SIGNATURE......................................

DATE ....

A sad reflection of the times when, even in moments of crisis, one must always be on guard.

Launching and Landing

In preparation for a trip, I work to a list pinned up where all my gear is stored. The person who remembers the lot on every trip is a better man than I. In time, a mental routine evolves. Even so, a quick look at the list when I think I've packed everything often shows something overlooked. After consulting the weather and everyone else concerned, if a trip is on, this is my routine: all fishing tackle, waders, waterproofs, extra clothes, safety tub, cameras, electrical gear, food and flasks form a big pile in the living room. Outside, the trailer board is fitted, outboard tank checked, bilge plugs fitted, and depending on which boat I am taking, a wooden support is put under the engine to secure it on tilt, or the small engine is locked in the car boot. Then it is time to fuel up the car and outboard if necessary. All packed, and having driven to the slade, first the boat is un-hitched, outboard removed from the car, trailer board put into the boot and the car parked up while the others fit the sounder, radio, and generally tidy up inside. I remove the straps before heading down the beach rather than risk stopping and getting bogged down at the water's edge. Once there push the trailer back end in first to the required depth, unclip the winch and gently shove her off. Many people have a short rope to hold in case the boat glides away into water too deep to reach. If you go for this idea, remember to either unclip or secure it before sailing, in case it gets wrapped around the propeller. With the boat in the water, someone has the lung splitting job of dragging the trailer back up beyond the high water line. It's odd, but trailers always appear to weigh heavier without the boat!

Getting ready for home is for the most part a reversal of the launching. While I go for the trailer, someone makes sure the boat just stays afloat. Some boats go back on their trailer better in a bit of water to maintain level. With flat bottomed boats it makes little difference. Butt the back rollers up to the boat, clip on the winch, flick the ratchet back into check, then, before cranking the handle, make sure no one is standing behind the winch in case the cable parts and whiplashes. Steel cables are especially vulnerable to this. As the bilge plug shows itself, remove and pocket it, letting any weight of water drain free, then it's back up the beach, sorting everything else out up top. Now the launch reversal can be completed. Back home, if it is late, any valuables are locked away for sorting out and cleaning, along with the boat, the following day. Eventually, everything is washed off and put back into its regular place. Both boat and trailer are brush hosed and the engine flushed, taking careful note of any damage. The anchor rope is neatly re-coiled inside the fish box. With the trailer lock clicked into position, it is back inside the house to sort out all the loose gear. Cameras, radio, compass and echo sounder get a wipe over. Terminal tackles are cut down to allow rod and reel cleaning, then all are re-tackled with new traces and a sharpened hook ready for next time. It may sound a bit of a drag, but eventually it becomes just another part of the game. Remember what was said earlier about actual fishing time taking only a small portion of any outing.

In between launch and retrieve, handling a boat at sea is very much like driving a car; what at first seemed perilously difficult, with experience develops into automated co-ordination, bordering on basic common sense. Though sea conditions can vary greatly, action taken in combating their effects is in the main, standard. Boat handling is as much about reading all the warning signs and taking evasive action, as knowing how to battle through a pitched sea. The signs are everywhere. Much of what affects the sea state is attributable to the action and inter-action of wind and tide. Understanding tidal movement will do much in improving all round ability.

Water may well appear to go in and out, but in reality, much of the time, tidal flow runs parallel to the shore, with the increasing or decreasing volume of water finding its own level, and giving a false impression. On our own stretch of coast, the Fylde, tides flood (move in) northwards, and ebb (move out) to the south. We, in common with much of western Britain, have to contend with a predominantly west to east airstream. For much of the time, we 'enjoy' a westerly blow, which does not do our inshore sea conditions a lot of good. Offshore winds come from the north east, east and south east, giving a flattening effect inshore. Out in the mid Irish Sea, it wouldn't matter much what the wind direction was; providing that it was strong, things would rough up. This explains why, even with an offshore breeze, conditions inshore may not be too good. The further one sails from the sheltered low water marks, the more exposed they become. Add to this, swell pushed in from the open sea, and it can get quite nasty. Where breezes are light and tides small, invariably it will be calm, though usually less so in winter than summer, when the least bit of a blow seems able to put up a big sea. It is on big tides, or with fresher breezes that problems really show themselves. Combine the pair and it gets decidedly nasty. For us a flood tide, which moves northwards, meeting an offshore north easterly breeze is worst in terms of potential discomfort on what should be a fishable day. Wind opposing tide creates a shallow choppy swell. Similarly, ebb tides opposed by south easterlies can become uncomfortable, but this is only around Lancashire. It may well differ elsewhere according to geographical positioning.

In fishing terms, flood tides very often outfish ebbs. Even so, if things look like being a little dodgey, go for the easy option and fish the ebb. Floods push harder than ebbs, particularly on big spring tides. Towards, and during high water, even on the calmest of days, there are usually a couple of awkward waves flopping onto the beach. As the sea state deteriorates, so the water's edge conditions follow suit. By fishing the ebb, the longer you are out, the better shore line conditions become, as the sea is rapidly shallowing along the water line, with more and more beach showing itself for landing upon. With top water edge swell still in mind, if you turn up at the slade to find a wall of surf blocking off the route to perfectly fishable water beyond, stick around. As the ebb gets underway, things may well improve. This brings us to the story of a boat attempting to launch in conditions such as these, but failing miserably. All the other boats happily out at anchor had put in earlier in the flood. Rather than wait, with water lapping the bottom of the slade and wall, in they went, only to have an engine failure a short way off. Back they came broadside on. That boat was knocked about for many a long while, the result being a total write off. Fortunately, they were insured.

What to do in bad conditions actually out at sea can be equally worrying. Here again, reading conditions can save the day. As the wind freshens, even if you do not pack up, at least have the good sense to move to a spot from which a quick home run is on the cards. If great grey sheets of cloud come pushing in from a seaward quarter, the probability of a good blow or squall is high. On lumpy, but fishable days, when at anchor, think very carefully before heading for shore. Consider the likelihood of rollers on the beach. Should these be a probability, try to land either before or after high water, but certainly not during without good reason. Big tides, as I say, throw up the worst edge conditions. They also fish well through top water and well into the ebb, so stick it out a while, catch a few more fish, and reduce the risks into the bargain. Inevitably, sooner or later, we all have to head in when conditions are bad. Heading in with a big swell, while you remain in deepish water away from waves with turning tops, all seaworthy boats over 13 feet, if handled correctly, should have little to fear. Most boating accidents occur within a couple of hundred yards from the shore. Heading into a swell, though bumpy and very wetting, if done at a reasonable speed should give few problems. Running in front of a swell is a less controllable and more hair raising experience. Each new wave looks destined to come rolling over the stern, then, just in time, the backend lifts and away you go like a surfboard until the wave overtakes you, leaving the boat seemingly motionless in a big grey hole, until the whole process repeats itself again and again. While surfing, control of the steering is difficult, but you must maintain sufficient power to run with the sea. Should you not, the boat moves broadside on, and over she goes. On the way in, tacking, or zig-zagging to get inshore without having to sail side on to the swell, should keep things safe. When it comes time to hit that beach, the swell should be running astern; keep it there. Beaching a boat properly, particularly for the beginner in these conditions, takes a lot of nerve. Get the crew up front to keep the bows digging in deep, pick a wave, open up the throttle, and run in with it. In a fast boat, be sure not to overtake your chosen wave, and under no circumstances ever consider a change of mind. Once committed, keep with it all the way in. If not, and the power is cut, water in transit hits the stern, turning the boat broadside to the swell, and again, over she will go. So never mind worrying about bits nicked out of the propeller or keel. Better a bit lost than everything. Smack that beach as hard as is necessary, with everyone out and up front pulling the boat up further the instant it touches, because the next roller will come right over the stern, swamping the lot. Worries about outboard damage can be laid to rest by setting the engine onto tilt. Heaven help anyone with a power tilt mechanism; do they risk turning the boat over by tilting too soon, or damage the propeller and transom by not doing so?

Another aspect of tidal action worth understanding is that the rate of flow within a tide is never constant. It will start off slowly, hit a mid flow peak, then progressively ease up. During the first hour, one twelfth of the water is moved; in the second hour two twelfths; in hours three and four, three twelfths each, then it slows down at the same gradual rate until eventually it turns. On big spring tides, so much water has to be shifted that no slack period between directional change occurs. The reverse is true of small neap tides which at best have hardly any discernible flow, followed by great slack periods at either end. Slack periods more often than not go hand in glove with poor fishing. On top of this, with the boat swinging at the mercy of the breeze, fishing can become a fruitless chore. It is far better to match fishing periods to the better stages of the tide. The trouble is, this too is not constant. Productive fish feeding bouts only occasionaly fall within office hours. Few consistently good anglers would expect to remain successful while rigidly adhering to a 9 to 5 schedule. Fish behave as they want.Recognise, then deal with this reality, and catches should improve accordingly. One of the major factors governing fish feeding behaviour is size and flow of a tide. Sadly, not all species react in the same way. Cod, for example, like plenty of run. They still feed, if briefly, on small tides but less get caught due to the reduced effective time factor. Here, the only really worthwhile period lies around hours three and four. Big tides promote the exact opposite. Useful run occurs throughout most of the tide, becoming too strong for easy feeding during hours three and four. What bites there are come at a hundred miles an hour. If they fail to connect, the fish is swept away before having a second go. Only as the tide eases, during top water, and for a couple of hours down can decent fishing be expected. During the fortnightly tide cycle, many grey areas of middle range tides also exist. These have a set of rules all to themselves. They are best fished in one complete direction. Experience will show when the tide becomes either too big or too small.

As weather affects sea conditions, it ultimately decides whether or not a trip can be fished. Weather is an all consuming word, covering many facets and extremes. For our purposes, the word weather means two things — wind and fog. Anything else, though it may affect our enjoyment, will have little bearing on our well being. The importance then of both gathering and understanding weather forecasts is paramount. Many forecasts these days are based on satellite pictures used to formulate an Atlantic chart. Britain lies in the path of a predominantly westerly air flow. Whatever we get is usually given birth somewhere east of the United States, developing, or more usually, deteriorating, en route for our shores. Low pressure, or depressions as they are also called, are the fellows to dread. High pressure, also known as anti-cyclones, more often than not give good fishing conditions and need only be watched for as opposed to critically watched. A low might go either way. Some, understandably are worse than others. These then are from where most dangers will spring, but to understand their effects, it is important that we first appreciate how they work. Pressure drops to its lowest at the centre of the depression, around which a spiral of moving air and cloud rotates, all heading inwards towards the eye. As the eye passes overhead, there may result a brief respite from the wind. Beware; do not misread this as the worst being over with and attempt putting to sea. As the system races overhead, within no time at all, things can be back to square one.

In the northern hemisphere, low pressures rotate anti-clockwise. Their usual form is to start developing somewhere out in mid-Atlantic, deepening markedly as they approach Ireland, after which most shoot northwards, just clipping the top north west corner of Scotland. This gives us our prevailing westerly winds. If however the low is persuaded, as some are, on into northern France, that anti-clockwise spiral of air can put us into easterly winds, the strength of which is always dependent upon the tightness of the isobars — lines drawn on a weather map showing places which have the same barometric pressure. Like contours on a map, isobars are mathematically spaced, separated by gaps of 4 millibars pressure. The deeper the low, the more rapid the gradient, and the closer the isobars are packed indicating strong winds. High pressure on the other hand, rarely has many isobars at all. Highs represent the exact opposite of lows in that their lighter winds are thrown outward from the centre with a clockwise rotation. In the main, winter high pressure stays well to the south of Britain, though if we are lucky, a nice big one will drift up plonking itself right on top of us, bringing clear skies, sharp frosts, and flat seas, and usually will take a lot of shifting. Any breeze associated with a high will be at its freshest towards the outer edge as air from it rises to infiltrate any adjacent low pressure in a vain attempt to bring about a pressure balance.

By way of an example, cast your eyes on the weather map of the British Isles. This is based on the normal pattern of things, with a low clipping

LOW
992
996
1000
1004
1008
1012
1016
1020
1024
1028
1032 *HIGH*

Scotland meeting a high lying over mid Europe. With an anti-clockwise rotation at the top, plus a clockwise rotation at the bottom, and a fair scattering of isobars, both are giving fairly stiff south westerly winds. This would offer poor prospects along western facing coasts, but reasonable possibilites in the east, which would be enjoying an offshore blow. However, if the high and low were to swap places, the whole situation would be reversed. Anglers on the east side would find themselves shorebound, while we in the west might be in with a chance. As our chart suggests quite a stiffish breeze, care would need to be exercised in not picking a wind against tide situation.

A number of options are open to the would be forecast seeker, perhaps the best known being the BBC shipping forecast. Being primarily aimed at aiding commercial vessels well offshore, it is not always the best forecast to relate to inshore small boat work. Neither is it always easily understood. It starts off like this .... "Here is the general synopsis issued by the meterological office at (time) on (day and date)." This word synopsis refers to the situation reguarding highs, lows and weather front movements at the time quoted, whereupon a general picture of the scene is painted. Following this, it goes into a regional breakdown, looking more closely at individual shipping areas starting with Viking, working around the coast and finishing at south east Iceland. You must then know what shipping area you intend to fish, which is not always the complete answer if it lies in a border region. When this is the case, listen out for both.

Let us take an example and expand it a little. 'Irish Sea — winds south westerly force 3 or force 4, locally force 5; rain at first; drizzle with mist later; visibility good becoming poor'. The wind then is averaging between 9 and 13 miles per hour according to the Beaufort scale. In short, a moderate south westerly. Locally five means coastal winds will average 18 miles per hour, which is fresh. This, when added to potentially poor visibility means that anyone contemplating fishing an exposed westerly facing coast shouldn't bother setting the alarm. Notice how a breeze can be fresher along the shore than further off. This is especially evident in warm summery weather when fresh shore line breezes can even differ in direction to the main predicted air flow. This happens because sea water holds its temperature, causing its warm layer of air to rise, drawing in replacement cooler air from over coastal sea water. At night, as the land cools more than the sea, warm air rises over the sea, drawing its replacement from the adjacent land. On summer days, cooling on-shore breezes occur. On summer evening, quite warm offshore breezes replace them.

Here is a summary of the most useful sources of gathering weather information to help plan a small boat trip. It should be noted that radio broadcast times may fluctuate, and should be checked against a current copy of the *Radio Times*. Telephone numbers may also alter. These can be checked by dialing 192 and enquiries. The local coastguard is also able to advise on current coastal conditions, as well as having up to the minute

SOUTH EAST
ICELAND

FAEROES

VIKING

NORTH UTSIRE

BAILEY

FAIR ISLE

HEBRIDES

FORTIES

SOUTH UTSIRE

CROMARTY

FORTH

FISHER

ROCKALL

MALIN

TYNE

DOGGER

GERMAN
BIGHT

IRISH SEA

HUMBER

SHANNON

LUNDY

THAMES

FASTNET

DOVER

PORTLAND

WIGHT

PLYMOUTH

SOLE

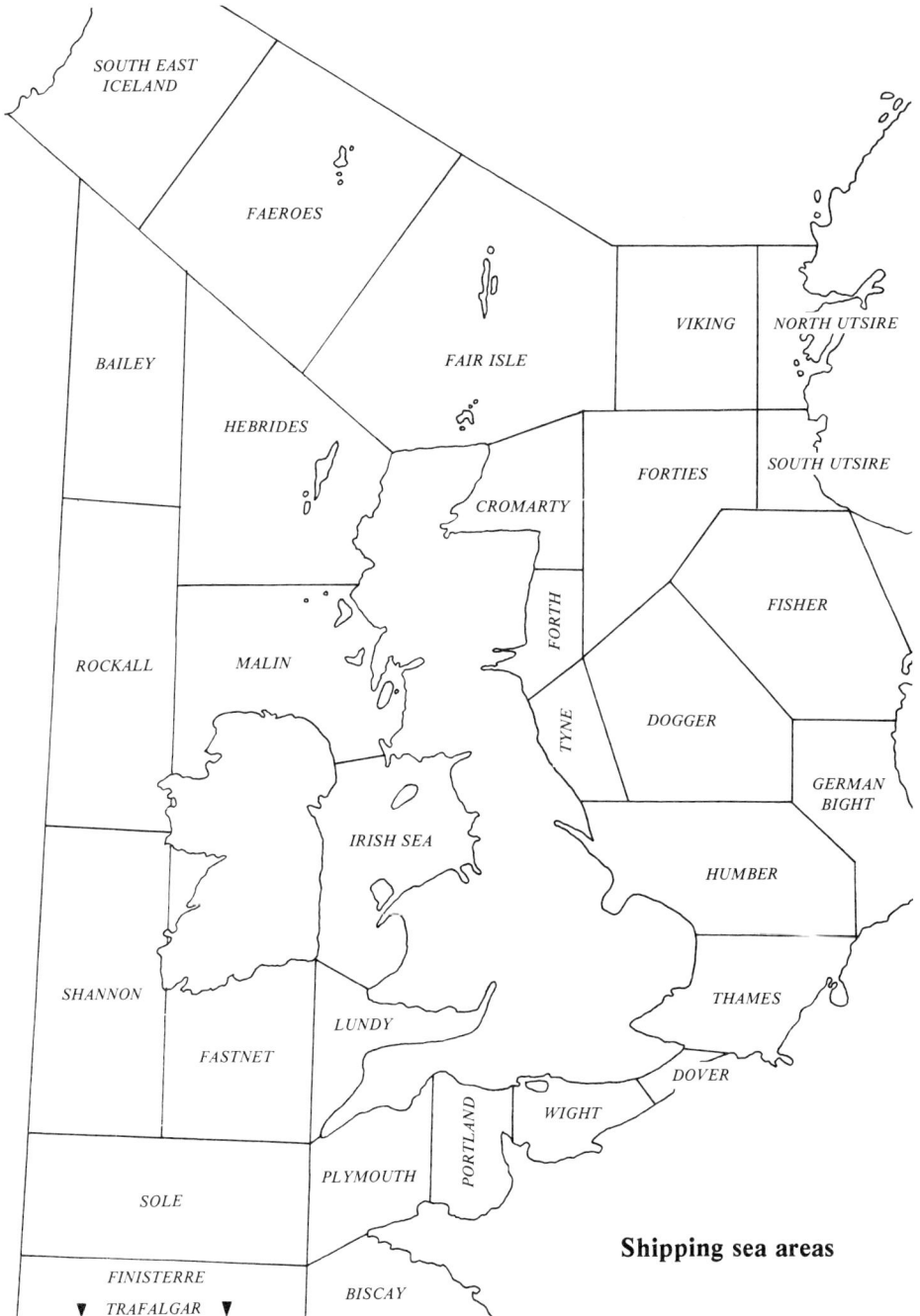

Shipping sea areas

FINISTERRE

▼ TRAFALGAR ▼

BISCAY

weather information. BBC TV weatherman showing the current chart after each news bulletin. BBC TV weatherman after Wednesday lunch time news gives the weekend chart and prospects. BBC TV weatherman Sunday lunch time with the coming week's prospects for farmers and growers. TV local weather reports after regional early evening magazine programme. Shipping forecast — longwave radio 4 on 15 metres or 20 kHz at 00.15, 06.25, 13.55 and 17.50. Round up of coastal weather report stations following on from the shipping forecast.

COASTGUARD RESCUE CENTRES

MRCC. ABERDEEN. Blaikies Quay, Aberdeen. Aberdeen (0224) 52334. MRSC. Shetland. Lerwick (0595) 2976. MRSC. Pentland. Kirkwall, Orkney. Kirkwall (0856) 3268. MRSC. Moray. Peterhead, Aberdeenshire. Peterhead (0779) 4278. MRSC. Forth. Fifeness, Crail, Fife. Crail (03335) 666. MRCC. YARMOUTH. Great Yarmouth, Norfolk. Great Yarmouth (0493) 51338. MRSC. Tyne. Tynemouth, North Shields, Tyne and Wear. North Shields (0632) 572691. MRSC. Humber. Spurn Point, near Hull, North Humberside. Spurn Point (09646) 351. MRCC. DOVER. Langdon Battery, Swingate, Dover, Kent. Dover (0304) 210008. MRSC. Thames. Hall Lane, Walton on the Naze, Frinton-on-Sea, Essex. Frinton-on-Sea (02556) 5518. MRSC. Shoreham. Shoreham-by-Sea, West Sussex. Shoreham (07917) 2226. MRCC. FALMOUTH. Castle Drive, Falmouth, Cornwall. Falmouth (0326) 317575. MRSC. Brixham. Brixham, Devon. Brixham (08045) 2156. MRCC. Solent. Totland Bay, Freshwater, Isle of Wight. Freshwater (0983) 752265. MRSC. Portland. Grove Point, Portland, Dorset. Portland (0305) 820441. MRCC. SWANSEA. Mumbles, Swansea, West Glamorgan. Swansea (0792) 66534. MRSC. Hartland. Hartland, Bideford, Devon. Hartland (02374) 235. MRSC. Milford Haven. Castle Way, Dale, Haverfordwest, Dyfed. Dale (06465) 218. MRSC. Holyhead. Holyhead, Anglesey. Holyhead (0407) 2051. MRSC. Liverpool. Crosby, Liverpool. Crosby (051) 931 3341. MRCC. CLYDE. Navy Buildings, Eldon Street, Greenock, Renfrewshire. Greenock (0475) 29988. MRSC. Ramsey. Ramsey, Isle of Man. Ramsey (0624) 813255. MRSC. Belfast. Bangor, Co. Down. Donaghadee (0247) 883184. MRSC. Oban. Boswell House, Argyll Square, Oban, Argyll. Oban (0631) 63720. MRSC. Stornoway. Stornoway, Isle of Lewis. Stornoway (0851) 2013.

MRCC....Maritime Rescue Co-ordination Centre.
MRSC....Maritime Rescue Sub Centre.

Inshore weather reports up to 12 miles....
BBC Radio 4 longwave 1500 metres or 200 kHz 00.20.
Small boat users forecast Radio 3 medium wave 247 metres or 1215 kHz Weekdays 06.55, Weekends 07.55.

Local radio stations transmit regular up to the minute local forecasts. Weatherline in the front of the telephone directory lists an assortment of local weather forecasting centres.

Beaufort Wind Scale.

Wind force	MPH	Wind	Sea
0	Under 1	Calm	like a mirror
1	1 - 3	light air	ripples without foam crests
2	4 - 7	light breeze	small wavelets
3	8 - 11	gentle breeze	large wavelets, crests begin to break about
4	12 - 18	moderate breeze	small waves; many white horses
5	19 - 24	fresh breeze	moderate waves; many white horses
6	25 - 31	strong breeze	light waves beginning to form white foam crests
7	32 - 38	near gale	sea heaps up white foam, begins to be blown in streaks
8	39 - 47	gale	moderate high waves of greater length; foam blown in well marked streaks.
9	48 - 54	strong gale	high waves; crests begin to topple and roll over. Spray may effect visibility
10	55 - 63	storm	very high waves; long overhanging crests; tumbling of sea becomes heavy and shocking
11	64 - 72	violent storm	exceptionally high waves; sea covered long patches of foam
12	73 - 81	hurricane	air filled foam and spray; sea completely white

Safety at Sea ·

If you do not normally wear a life jacket at all times, for your own good, at least put one on when working close to the shore line with a fair sea running. For us to say you must wear one is out of the question. Of course we recommend it, but we also recognise the fact that adults will make their own decisions. Hopefully, what we say will count for something. Floatation suits, as well as being warm, provide a safety factor, as do neoprene wet suits, uncomfortable as they often are. The wearing of waders, though necessary during launch and retrieve, is not good policy out at sea. Far better to have an old pair of trainers or deck shoes for the summer to change into, and thermally insulated moon boots for the colder weather. Always carry sufficient warm clothing. You can never carry too much, whereas too little could ruin the day. In the winter, amongst other things, I wear a thermal vest and long johns, though I would dread being un-wrapped in hospital were I to have an accident with some of the other 'extras' I wear! Gloves and a hat are essential, particularly the latter, as vast quantities of heat pass skywards through uncovered heads. Good woollen jumpers worn in layers trap heat best. In the event of a capsize, though cold water still reaches the body, layers of wool will stave off rapid body heat loss. The biggest fear amongst most boaters seems to be that of drowning. People feel that by wearing a lifejacket no harm can come to them. Certainly, assisted buoyancy is crucial, but all is far from safe. Straightforward drowning as the cause of death in small boat tragedies is rare, even though it may be the eventual outcome.

Hypothermia brings about the circumstances under which many drownings become inevitable. This then is the main problem to beat. The sea being vast and cold, draws away body heat in an attempt to effect a temperature balance. With a body core temperature of around 90 degrees F, you become as though under the influence of alcohol. A survey undertaken some years ago amongst yachters discovered that the majority of people lost at sea could in fact swim, which may well have made a direct contribution to their death, while many non-swimmers were saved. In some cases, the swimmers had decided to make for shore. Having got part way, they became too fatigued either to press on, or make it back to their upturned boat. The result is sadly obvious. Over confidence kills. Swimming is also a drain on vital body heat. So long as you remain buoyant, either by wearing a lifejacket and/or by clinging to the upturned hull, stay put. Often those poor terrified souls unable to swim, left clinging to anything floating for dear life, outlast everyone else. Firstly, by not getting themselves drowned, but more importantly, by managing to beat off hypothermia for long enough to be rescued; not that careful dinghy anglers should end up swimming in the first place. Yachters see taking a regular dip as part of their game; I for one do not share their enthusiasm.

Navigation

I would doubt there is a subject so potentially complex, yet so funda-mentally essential to all putting to sea in boats as finding your way around the place. Without signposts and pathways, navigation can be the great thorn in the side of many, particularly those like us whose sole purpose for the sailing is not geared simply to an enjoyment of being afloat. We have been presented with the task of performing something of a literary balancing act for while we need to maximise the extent of information given, we must at the same time not get so 'heavy' as to frighten anyone away. Hopefully then, our high wire compromise will suit all basic needs. Fortunately, conditions allowing, in our branch of sailing, we for the most part fish within sight of land. The fact that land might suddenly disappear from view in conditions of poor visibility is a reality we must accept and be prepared to deal with. Basic navigation relies on the ownership of, ability to use, and complete trust in, a decent compass. Size and cost are immaterial. So long as it is reliable and simple to use, both of which do not always go hand in glove with big spending, few problems will arise. Before wading into the whole thing, it might be best to iron out a few minor points to reduce confusion.

A compass needle or pointer is always attracted to magnetic north, which lies irritatingly a few degrees away from true north. For our purposes, unless readings are being taken from, or transferred to a chart, it is sufficient to work only with magnetic north (as read from the compass). Take what you have got and make full use of it. If you intended circum-navigating the globe on a port to port basis, it might be worth delving deeper. But for working a straight line back to shore in fog, north is north. The next point also concerns fog. For point to point distance navigation, unless accurately chart plotted, the line between A and B will not be a straight one, due to the effects of wind and tide, neither of which are constant. With as little as a one knot tide running at right angles to a moving boat, if you sail for 30 minutes, it is possible to be up to half a mile off course. So complex and space consuming is the explanation required to put charted navigation across to an audience unable to ask questions, particularly concerning the conversion of magnetic to true north and visa versa, that we intend to give the subject a miss. To gain any sort of meaningful appreciation calls for a proper course at a nautical college, but let me stress that conversion is only necessary for chart work.

Over short distances, though wind and tide working to throw a boat off course will affect precise navigation, providing you are not sailing naturally obstacle ridden waters, straight line sailing taking north to be just that as shown on the compass will be accurate enough for anglers wanting simply to make it back to shore. In most cases, though not all, fog coincides with fairly breeze conditions. Little wind makes for settled seas, which in turn allows you to open up the throttle, unless it's a real pea souper. By covering distances in a shorter space of time, the effect of tidal push is minimised. Speaking of motoring at full throttle, some compasses are not designed for either speed, or a buffeting sea. Be sure and buy a well dampened straight forward non gimbled variety. Actual choice has been fully explained in the ancilliary equipment section. What was not elaborated upon was compass useage. We recommend a model in a fixed, bracketed housing with a small forward viewing window showing just that part of the rose (calibrated head) which happens to be floating past the read-off point at a given time. Though they have their drawbacks, on the whole this type is best suited to dinghy angling. What basically happens is that as the boat turns, taking with it the fixed housing, so the rose remains attracted to north, allowing the case to move around it bringing the actual direction in which the boat is pointing, to the display point and read-off mark. Where this style of compass lets itself down is in not showing the entire rose at all times. For safety's sake, any angler while sailing out should note the course being taken, to be reversed for the home leg, but this too can have its drawbacks. It is rare indeed to head out in a dead straight line without total concentration. No straight line having been sailed out means nothing to be reversed for the sail back. But without doubt the greatest bugbear comes when, while fishing at anchor, fog starts to come down, not having taken any sort of reading at all. To then get a reading, the boat has to be pointed back towards the launching spot, meaning up-anchoring, which a lot of people will be loathe to do. So before putting down the anchor, it will be necessary to turn the bows back towards shore for a reading. That is of course unless you carry insurance — a small hand compass. As recommended earlier, I carry a Silva orienteering compass in my jacket pocket. Its needle, as one might expect, points to north. The calibrated outer rim rotates until 'N' lines up with the needle. As the entire rose is visible, a quick reading can be taken with the anchor still down. Heading back on that reading is done later on the big fixed compass. A small hand compass is also useful in confirming the accuracy of the other during a shoreward journey in which land seems a long time showing., Okay, it might not be as accurate as big brother, but rather than leave you thinking, 'I can't be bothered up-anchoring; besides, I know where land is', it will ensure that feet be placed back onto dry land somewhere with the trailer quite close by.

Throughout the boating section, we have tried to take the realistic view that while it is at times not always advisable to do some of the things that anglers undoubtedly do, our ignoring the fact will not make the practice go away. Do not misconstrue our recognition as acceptance or justification. We merely give their actions the occasional airing not as encouragement to others, but to point out what has become bad practice, its pitfalls, and possible ways of averting disaster should you too fall into the trap. Learn from mistakes by all means, but preferably those made by others, which sometimes end up labelled as 'the ultimate'. With this in mind, let me outline a way of at least finding land with a watch, a tide table and a scrap of paper for those fool enough to be caught out in fog with nothing else. Ask any boat load of anglers in fog to point out land, and I wager you will get a different answer from each. In some cases, you'd need a big fuel tank and immigration papers if you handed over the helm! Were I to be caught out off Cleveleys, a look at my watch and tide table would tell me the stage of the tide. For this, prior knowledge of the direction your flood and ebb tides run is essential. Along the Fylde, it floods to the north and ebbs to the south. Let us say it is half flood. By dropping a piece of paper into the water and watching it move, I know where north lies, and can subsequently work out the direction of east, which to us means land. Never rely on the stern pointing exactly at the flow of the tide. Should a stiff breeze be cutting across the flow, estimations could end up miles out.

Getting around without signposts in the dull grey sameness brought about by bad visibility is probably the only time we will travel wearing a metaphorical blindfold, and as such is perhaps the only time most of us ever bother with the compass outside of attempting with its help to locate fish. It can be un-nerving to say the least when a heavy visibility blanket comes down while fishing is under way. Any one of a number of reasons can lie behind it, including a summer sea mist, heat haze, frost haze, freezing fog, drizzle and heavy snow. Consider the likelihood of these before motoring off relying solely on 'the visible' for getting about. And be very sure of yourself before deciding to head out deliberately into the hidden grey yonder. Undertaken with care, sailing out into fog is possibly less hazardous than pushing back to shore. Given that the man on the tiller is sure no permanent obstruction will do his hull a mischief, the only thing to worry about is colliding with another boat, particularly if it is likely to weigh several thousand tons more than you. So go to sea in fog with great care if you feel you must. Personally, I prefer not to, and feel sure the powers that be would strongly recommend the same. Being caught out, particularly in winter, is quite something else. With fog from the onset, as you don't really know exactly where your favourite fishing spot is because of a lack of land marks, it does not hurt to concentrate every effort in running a straight course. If you don't, how else can you be sure of a straight run back? In addition, time the duration of your seaward run so as to know when to expect 'hitting' shore on the return.

Timing a seaward run also has relevance for navigating in areas when the fishing takes place at a point where the launching ramp is obscured from view such as around a headland. Navigating to the far side of a headland involves a two leg course, each leg running more or less parallel to the shore, but sufficiently far enough out to ensure safe water. Time the sail out to a point where both the launch site and proposed fishing mark can be seen and checked simultaneously with the compass, noting the time taken to reach the point and the reading back to the trailer. For the next leg, time a compass course to the mark. Now, if fog descends, sail a timed reversal of the last course back to the change-over point, and the second leg back to the slip. Again, keep a check on the timing so as to know when to expect the shore coming into sight.

In theory, this sounds easy. In practice, it may prove not only difficult, but hazardous in that it makes no allowance for the potential margin of error forced by the effects of wind and tide throwing the timing out, which could lead to a premature second leg, and disaster on the rocks. The only way to be sure of getting it absolutely right is to sit down with a set of parallel rules, a chart and calculating pad, which, as we all know, is not always possible in a small open boat. So with any threat of poor visibility on the cards, give dual leg navigation a miss.

There are occasions when, because of a good catch, you might want to give a spot another try at some future date; not that it will necessarily

IALA System A

Port

Red

Green

Starboard

Lights colour

4

Any

Rhythm

Any

4

Both

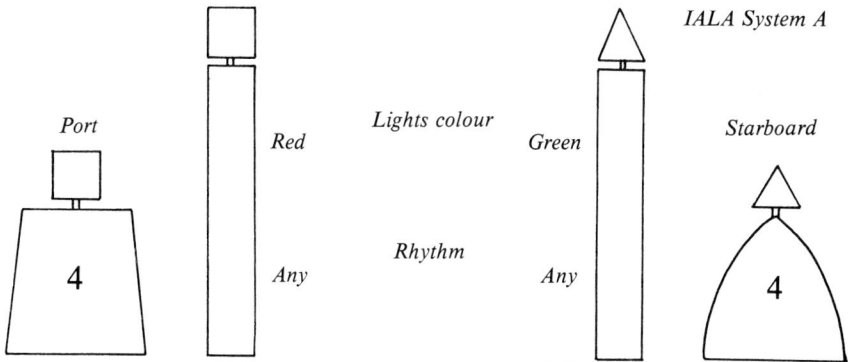

Lateral (Fairway) buoys
Can or pillar shape with red flashing
light showing any rhythm.

Conical or pillar shape, green or
occasionally black. Green light with
any rhythm.

Colour key: (both diagrams) Port side: all red, Starboard side: all green

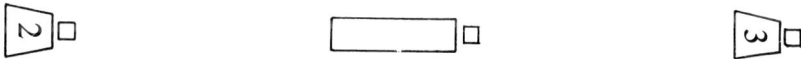

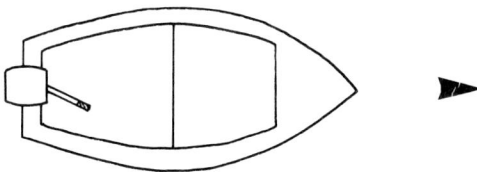

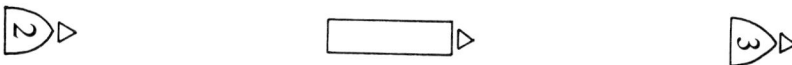

The above buoys are used in clearly defined channels as shown.

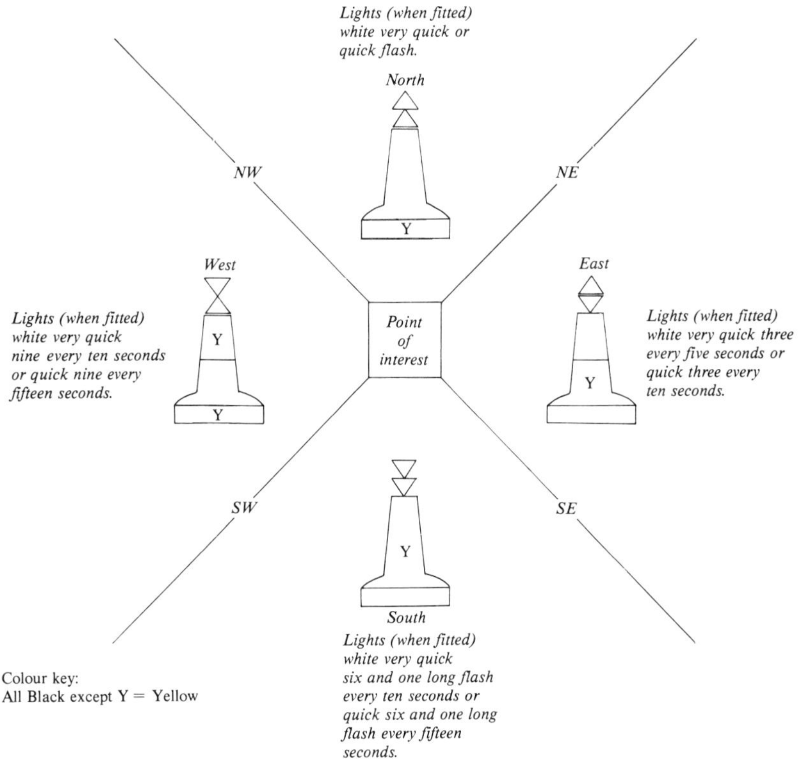

Lights (when fitted)
white very quick or
quick flash.

North

NW

NE

West

East

Lights (when fitted)
white very quick
nine every ten seconds
or quick nine every
fifteen seconds.

Point
of
interest

Lights (when fitted)
white very quick three
every five seconds or
quick three every
ten seconds.

SW

SE

South

Lights (when fitted)
white very quick
six and one long flash
every ten seconds or
quick six and one long
flash every fifteen
seconds.

Colour key:
All Black except Y = Yellow

Cardinal buoys: these are used in conjunction with a compass, and mark a given point of interest or hazard. It can be a spar or pillar type, and guards the four gradients. Your position in relation to the hazard is given by arrangement of cones on top. Light sequence (when fitted) as shown above.

produce the goods to order a second time. I have seen people who, after all but filling the boat with cod, put over a marker buoy returning the next day only to blank, while others nearby caught. Be sure you were no more than lucky enough to be in the right spot at the right time, never to be repeated again. However, if your new found hot spot does turn out to be consistently productive, quite naturally, you will want to return not only regularly, but with ease. To do this, you will need to be able to pick up prominent land marks such as factory chimneys, pylons, cooling towers and the like back on shore. It can be done with two landmarks, but is better with three, one of which should be known to you anyway, it being the point of launch. One either side of this completes the trio. Get a compass bearing for each down on paper. Next time out, sail seaward on the bearing from the ramp (reverse the reading of that taken while out at sea) until the other two land marks line with their respective positions on the compass rose. With a standard

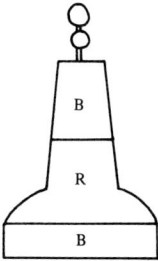

Isolated danger buoy
To warn of small isolated dangers such as submerged rocks or a wreck. Illuminated by a white light group flashing rhythm.

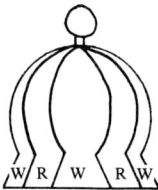

Safe water buoy
Denote navigable water all round. Used as mid channel marker or centre line mark. Can be either spherical, pillar or spar. White light isophase occulting or 1 long flash every 10 seconds.

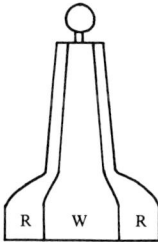

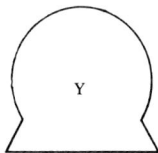

Special mark buoy
Not necessarily a navigational aid. Individual special features identified by chart consultation. Can be any shape other than those shown. Yellow light. Rhythm determined by other buoys in the area so as not to conflict.

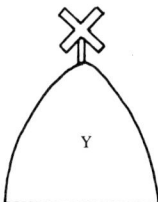

Colour key: B = Black, R = Red, W = White, Y = Yellow

compass as already recommended, this will prove difficult, even impossible. It won't prove that much easier if it is to be done accurately on any other compass, unless it has been designed specifically for this job. What is needed is a hand bearing compass. Buying one of these will make all navigation work easier, even cutting out any need to install a sailing compass in the first instance. When using a standard compass for picking up land marks, it can be difficult to get even a reasonable reading in a pitching boat as the compass cannot be lined up properly and read. By using a prism, the hand bearing compass marker is lined up with the object back on shore and the instrument read without ever removing it from in front of your eye. Even with this, do not expect miracles. If you've ever been out on a wreck fishing trip, you will understand just how difficult perfect navigation, even with electronic aids, is. These boats intercept longtitudinal and latitudinal radio signals with a Decca navigator, yet still have to quarter the selected area searching for the wreckage on the echo sounder. We cannot hope to match that sort of accuracy.

Charts are of exceptional use when it comes to gaining an awareness of the geographical layout lying beneath the hull. A chart is a map if you like, full of abbreviations and specific signs, with some 500 or so regional offerings covering all British coastal waters. Different marked buoys for example have specific jobs and meanings. Depths nowadays are no longer quoted in fathoms, having gone metric, and are shown in metres below chart datum, which, in layman's terms, means the depth measured at low water on the lowest astronomical tide. Actual depths therefore are calculated by adding the depth of the tide prevailing, taken at a specific time from the tide table. Depths are dotted all over the place, as indeed are small abbreviations concerning sea bed texture. Prominent land marks visible from the sea are correctly positioned along the obligatory piece of coastline shown, though sadly, launching facilities, except for harbours, are not. These charts are compiled and constantly updated by the people of the Royal Hydrographic Department who, in addition to distributing their findings for sale through numerous chandlery outlets, have also produced a key to all their symbols and abbreviations compacted into one additional small chart or booklet number 5011.

Finally, the reader should be aware that it is an offence to make fast to a navigation buoy for the purpose of fishing or to anchor in such a position as to impede regular traffic up a channel or fairway.

SECTION TWO

PRACTICAL FISHING

With few exceptions, the species taken by shore and charter boat rods are just as much a possibility from a small boat. Do not run away with the idea that they are necessarily a probability. Habit and limited distribution amongst some species may see them scarce even where access is not limited, but rare indeed are the fish listed in the British record list not to have put in at least a limited showing inshore. Within certain boundaries, small boats often outfish everyone else taking tackle down to the sea. What we do is fill a niche, and as such should neither become blasé about the good times, nor depressed when others elsewhere do better. Accept what is given with gratitude.

There have been instances when dinghy rods have hauled aboard ton-up skate, a halibut, even the thresher shark record weighing in at 323lbs. Surprises and oddities will greet us all at some stage of the day, otherwise we continue in trying to get the best under our own steam from the more mundane. Here then is a look through the eyes of two dinghy fanatics at the forty most likely fish to come from British inshore marks during the normal course of things, along with suggestions as to what should or should not be done once they hit the deck. Terminal tackle set-ups are described where necessary and drawings of these appear at the end of this section.

Cod

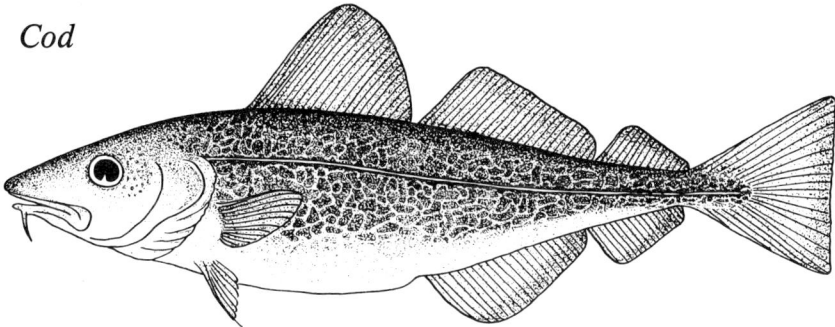

Cod – Gadus morhua: the three dorsal and two anal fins are a feature of this family of fishes. So too is the chin barbel. Separating it from the similar relatives is done by the colouration and markings. Colouration can vary according to terrain, ranging from reddish to green, and more commonly, sandy brown. A very pronounced white lateral line and mottled back and upper sides aid identification.

Cod represent to many sea anglers just what fishing is all about; a sort of foundation stone upon which obsessions are built. Though I am probably as guilty as anyone, I cannot for the life of me understand why we get so excited when the cod appear. Other fish grow bigger, fight better, even taste nicer. None the less, cod do have an ability to wind up the emotions of even the most placid dinghy men. Thankfully, it is a very widespread species available to the vast majority of us. Dependent of course on just exactly where you live, or more to the point, where you are willing to trail your boat, opportunities are going to differ greatly. Nobody lives too far away from some cod-holding bit of sea. Perhaps this, allied to their potential for growth and at times very obliging feeding habits, is the big attraction.

Over on the east coast from around mid Yorkshire northwards, cod provide rich pickings all summer long, perhaps even more so than in the early part of winter. For the rest of us, cod are considered a backend and winter prospect, which isn't necessarily always the case. Blinkered thinking encouraged by short sighted writing in the past is to blame for that one.

True, for the most part, most cod forsake the areas so beloved in winter, but they have to go somewhere. Many meander way offshore, frequenting deep water wrecks. Summer feeding is very much different from that of the cooler months. Inshore reefs and kelp beds provide a healthy larder of peeling crabs, small fishes and the like and cod both know and exploit this situation. Proximity to shore is of no real consequence. Water depth allied to the extent of feeding appear to have the greatest bearing. The heavier and deeper lying the ground, the better, but to fish a bait hard on the bottom would be asking for trouble. Over extensive kelp beds, drifting is the key to locating feeding groups, saving the option of short drifts, or even anchoring when a concentration of fish is found. Hooks really need to be strung out above the weight on short droppers, preferably with the weight, or chrome lure if you prefer, fixed to the trace with a lower breaking strain of nylon to minimise tackle losses in the event of a hang up. To the droppers tie baited hooks, feathers, or muppets (coloured plastic squids) all of which take fish, particularly as summer seas are very much cleaner on the whole. Jigging too is a highly efficient way of exploiting a heavy ground potential. It is also physically tiring. For this reason why not bait all the lures, even the jig treble? Not only does bait give the rig additional pulling power, it allows you to take a breather and still be in with a chance of fish.

To put accurate arrival and departure schedules down in black and white is impossible. Cod come and go at vastly differing times, dependent to a large degree on availability of food. Only one other factor commits them to a real time table, and that is their spawning cycle. The one common denominator with cod distribution is that smaller fish seem to make the inshore marks first, some never leaving until they are mature. On all but the north sea dinghy marks, this usually begins sometime during the autumn. Better fish slowly swell the ranks, backed up by the slow plodding jumbos towards the turn of the year. A combination of two factors lies behind the shoreward migration. From late March to April, the mature fish are going to be called upon to seed future stocks, a very rigorous pursuit at best. Building roes calls for much concentrated feeding and just beyond the low water mark is a very good place to get it. Funnily enough, many North Sea cod do the whole thing in reverse. Their main spawning grounds are close to the Dogger Bank in the southern North Sea. Fish that are happy feeding within a few miles of the shoreline all the summer must undertake quite a swim to make the grounds in time, leaving in the main, small immature fish inshore for the winter sport. Of course, the further south and consequently closer to the Dogger Bank one fishes, the longer the mature fish are likely to linger inshore. A look at the early winter sport along the Suffolk beaches, and tremendous dinghy and charter fishing from the Essex ports looking out into the Thames is proof enough. Cod like to move inshore for as long as time permits, cleaning up the many shrimps, sprats, bullheads, prawns, pout, shellfish, worms and crabs to be found as close to shore as dropping winter temperatures will permit. Not that all cod necessarily move in on the low water mark as the single great provider of food. Some get involved in exploiting the eco-systems set up by the wrecks. For the most part, wrecks lie in deep water well out of small boat range, though not always. Other cod shoal up on offshore banks, but in the main, we small boaters have as good a chance as anyone of picking up the biggest prizes, particularly as by the very nature of the boats we use in shallow water we are given a head start.

Often, shallow water means coloured water, stirred by an endless stream of winter gales and squalls. With this in mind, baits are best chosen to exploit the very keen sense of taste and smell employed by cod. In such conditions, lures are a waste of time, needing clear water with well grouped fish to justify the effort. The odd thing about cod is that they can be very parochial in their precise feeding habits. In general terms, just about anything that moves represents food of sorts to a hungry cod. Yet in specific areas, one particular bait will outfish everything else put down, only to be ignored when tried elsewhere. As examples, mid North Sea cod are fond of mussel and ragworm. Along the eastern channel, sprats will catch fish, but not off Lancashire where blacklug is the killer. Cod feeding around the Solent entrances prefer big squids, while west country fish take lures and fish baits. Scottish cod go for lures on account of the clear deep water, with the best natural baits including shellfish and worms. Try wherever possible to find out any particular local preference, and remember that these are not absolute. Any big juicy bait has to be in with a chance. Very probably the best all rounder for cod popularity is lugworm.

My own native Fylde coast is as good an example of shallow water codding as any. Conforming as it does to the general pattern, we find our fish over a scattering of boulders and stones. Specific marks, save for few gullies up which fish run, despite what people may say, simply do not exist. Patience allied to the right approach is the key to success. It is what goes onto the hook, how often it is changed, and how it is presented that matters.

When the anchor goes down, allow a little time for things to settle out. Constant moves are no good to anyone. In such conditions baits need to be fished smack on the bottom. Isolated instances of all sorts of baits and terminal tackle catching fish do occur, but it is consistency that is the yardstick. Nothing exploits a bottom feeder better than a simple flowing trace. Ours usually match the rod length. With swivel against the end eye, the hook clips onto the reel spacer bar. Hook sizes vary according to baits. It is no use trying to thread tiny blow lug onto a big 6/0. Conversely, a 2/0 hidden inside a whole squid would have precious little chance of burying

Brian and Bob Douglas with three Fylde coast jumbo cod.

home. Our early season cod run perhaps to 10 pounds and get half a blacklug covering a 2/0. As the fish get bigger 4/0s take over, finally moving up to 6/0s and as much lug as possible when the big fish arrive. A 20lb fish is a prize; a 30 pounder huge.

We find fishing to be at its best when the baits are trotted downtide over the stern. Most local charter boats find it very difficult indeed to get anywhere near the dinghies for either quantity or quality. Cod in shallow water are susceptible to boat noise. For this reason, a smaller boat is a passport to greater opportunity. Bradwell charter skippers John Rawle and Bob Cox proved to the angling world that huge catches are possible from shallow water charter boats, providing the baits are worked beyond the influence of disturbance. As dinghies give only minimal noise from rope turbulence and hull slap, and they carry fewer potential noise makers on board, casting need not be so distant. And as all the rods used can comfortably be accommodated over the stern, there is no need to be holding across the tide in true uptide tradition. In fact, a simple down tide trot will do equally well. However, getting a take is one thing; dealing with it is something else. With plenty of line out, a fickle tug the moment the rod tip twitches won't even be felt down at the business end. Pick up the rod when a bite registers, and point the tip at the fish, taking in any slack line. Now wait and really feel it thumping away. Then drive the hook home in a full arm's length sideways arc, again taking in the slack line as the rod is lowered back to a reeling position. Keep the drag fairly lightly set. If you are not gaining line, apply pressure to the spool with the thumb during the upward lift of pumping, repeated after taking on line when lowering the rod. Steady pressure soon sees the fish ready for boating without any risk of either ripping the hook free or parting the line should it decide on a sudden departure back to the bottom. Thumbs can quickly release spool tension; over-tight star drags cannot.

Whiting

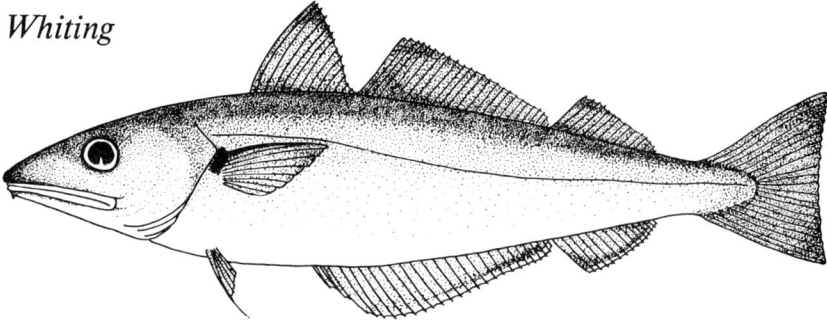

Whiting – Merlangius merlangus: upper jaw distinctly longer than the lower, with only a very small barbel. The origin of the first anal fin is under the mid point of the first dorsal fin. Not as deep bodied as the pouting, nor mottled like the cod. Colouration: dark greenish brown on the upper back, becoming golden, then silvery beneath. There may be some faint golden flecks on the flanks.

Whiting are hardly fish to be given too much time or attention if there is anything better on the cards, yet are fish without whose presence, the very aspect of small boat fishing would be much poorer. An abundant and totally reliable little fish whose backend to early winter shoreward migration is legendary. Granted, some areas are fortunate in having some whiting over much of the year; for the rest of us, it is a waiting game. Often it is said that the forerunners appear inshore with the first frosts. But what about mild winters when coastal frosts just don't materialize? Still the whiting make the scene. Actual seabed water temperatures vary little with the ups and downs of air temperatures. Down there it is a far more gradual affair, affected only by prolonged rises and falls. How then might the whiting know it is frosty on shore? The truth of the matter is, they do not. The link lies in the fact that whiting actively dislike turbulent water conditions, only coming into really shallow water when the sea is flat. Calm seas often go hand in glove with light winds and high pressure, which in turn means clear skies and inevitably, frost.

Try and recall some of your best whiting sessions. Mine more often than not have been on starry nights with a big bright full moon and the cold numbing fingers and toes as the boat sits motionless on a glassy sea. Certainly darkness sharpens their appetites extending their activities to within casting range of even the beach, meaning that after dark, distance out is not a crucial factor.

Over much of Britain, whiting make a forceful show during October, peaking in November, followed by numerical decline towards the end of the year. Individuals however hit a conditional peak towards the end of their stay, with rich pickings having put much meat on the scrawny frames of several weeks earlier.

Usually, clean sandy ground is favoured, though quite a few of the whiting I catch these days are taken while cod fishing over the stones. In some seasons, such catches become quite numerous, but can only be considered as overspill from the adjacent sands. Two categories of bait in the main do the same damage, worms and small fish strips. Whiting feed very close to bottom, and probably on it for much of the time. Yet a worm bait put amongst them on a flowing trace for cod won't take a fraction of the fish caught on the same bait offered a couple of inches higher.

Bottom dapping baits given movement by the flow of the tide, or the roll of the boat, are very successful. A number of terminal presentations spring to mind. More or less any with snoods fixed above the weight will catch. French booms and linked nylon snoods do this particularly well, with hooks around 2/0 being ideal. Unfortunately, these rigs share one common fault. In the tidal flow, all snoods swing in the same direction necessitating either spacing the hook lengths much more carefully to avoid tangles, or using short stiff snoods. Either way, only one hook will be exploiting the bottom

A brace of whiting taken on a paternoster and mackerel bait.

Fewer but bigger whiting are picked up accidentally on bottom fished cod baits.

dapping angle, that is unless you use a metal boomed paternoster. Old fashioned looking Christmas trees they may well be; efficient at spreading a number of baits across the same level they most certainly are. Shop bought paternosters in the main come with three booms. My preference is for two. This is achieved either by cutting the odd boom free, or by using the purchase as a pattern to copy with eighth gauge brass wire, neglecting to put in the upper arm. An instructional diagram appears with the terminal rigs later on.

Whiting are fish of feeding moods and sometimes, using fish strips, you will fill a boat. On other occasions, mackerel, herring and sprats are given a very cool reception. Worm then is top of the menu for the day. I think fish strips probably work better after dark when whiting are totally reliant upon following scent trails. It doesn't take a lot at night to work a shoal into a feeding frenzy. Forget casting well away from the boat. Whiting are never shy fish even at their most fickle. Fish of up to 2lbs seem commonplace. Anything topping 3lbs is very good, becoming progressively scarcer as they approach the 6¾ pound record. Consistency in repeatedly hitting the same spot is what it is all about. No point bringing fish onto the boil at one spot, only to cast the bait elsewhere. The nearer the boat, the greater the accuracy. If possible, get them going immediately astern. Tugs and rattles continue with even the merest hint of bait left on the hook. Miss a bite and it doesn't matter. Drop straight back and up things start again. Worm baits do not have the frenzying effect. Still, you have to give the fish what they want and take what comes up. And when they do in big numbers, try not to be swept along by the general euphoria of the thing. Even a fish apparently so numerous as whiting can be prone to over-exploitation. Already the commercial sector is looking hard at the viability of whiting as an up and coming table fish. We can hardly condemn others when we allow ourselves to be drawn into an overkill situation. Enjoy the catching by all means, but just think before you kill. Try them on light tackle, they are great fun.

You can always tell when someone has had a good whiting catch. Look for the cuts and scratches along the finger ends. You'll quickly notice your own when the salt water hits them. Small though the whiting's teeth are, they can break your skin while removing the hook.

Pouting

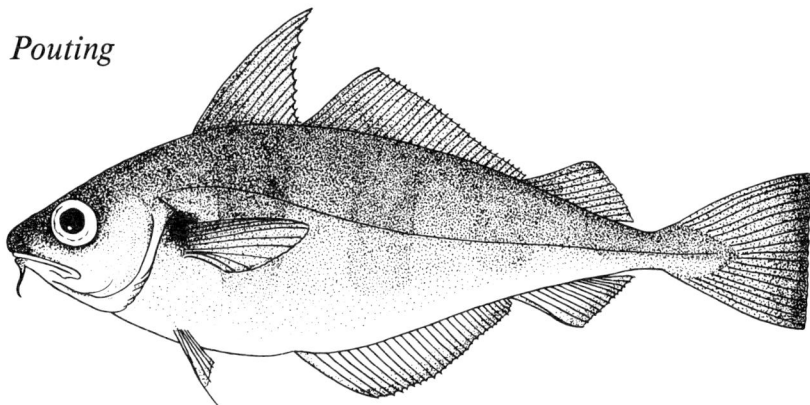

Pouting – Trisopterus luscus: quite a deep bodied fish whose fins are so close as to almost overlap. At the base of the pectoral fin is a prominent black spot. Colouration can vary with terrain. Though generally a coppery brown with distinct darker bands running down the flanks, it may well have a purple sheen.

Much of what holds for catching whiting is equally true for pouting. Just a few seasonal and distributional differences separate the pair. The pouting is a much less well received fish, more often than not viewed as little more than a bait robber. None the less, pouting on more than one occasion may have the dubious honour of providing the only stepping stone between failure and success. Over broken heavy ground, they go about their bait robbing throughout the summer and early winter, until dropping inshore temperatures push them off to where fluctuations are much less likely. By and large a fish, seeing a small boat inshore, marks it as its shallow water limit. Rare indeed are pouting taken from the beach. Offshore reefs can provide them by the sackfull, with some very large specimens into the bargain.

Night congering out from Looe we used to pick up some fair specimens pushing 3lbs, though not as big as those taken bream fishing around the rock pinnacles further out towards the Eddystone. The record itself is a west country fish of 5½lbs taken off Berry Head. In the main, not a deliberate target for most serious dinghy men. Still, I must bow to those who want them, requesting they take my share as well. Again, paternostered worm or fish strips do well. Shellfish are also taken with relish. A string of baited mackerel feathers is a reliable method, though where smaller fish persist, hooks should be a little smaller, say down to size 1. One way in which they do differ from whiting is in showing no reluctance in having a go at baits lying on the bottom. Here I am thinking of precious cod baits which they rip to pieces and totally destroy, unable to get their lips around a big 6/0.

The pouting is a rather more delicate fish than whiting, very easily damaged by rough handling. It is also prone to compression problems if brought up quickly from even moderately deep water, big bulging eyes being the tell-tale sign. In our area we call them 'Martys' after the funnyman Marty Feldman and his not dissimilar facial expression. One thing in their favour, is that they can make good whole baits for tope, conger and bass, but the trouble is, when you want a small one you can never catch the damn things.

Poor Cod

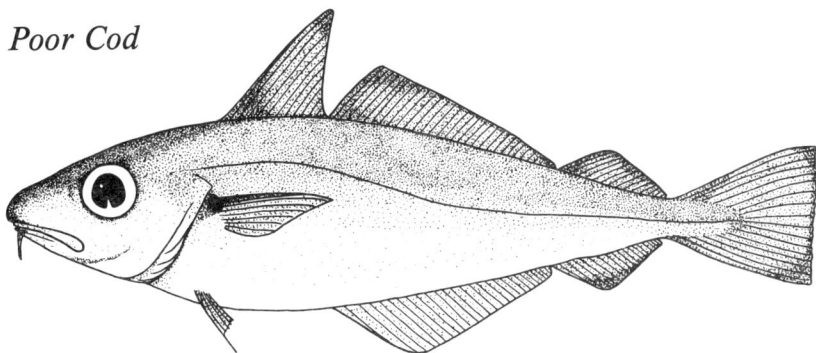

Poor Cod – Trisopterus minutus: similar to, though bodily less deep than, a small pouting. The pelvic fins reach just past the vent. The origin of the first anal fin lies opposite the gap between the first two dorsal fins. Colouration: golden yellowish brown. A delicate little fish prone to loss of scales when handled. No banded flank markings.

On occasion, these small fish are going to get caught mixed in with pouting over heavy ground. Despite the fact that my boat has the dubious honour of holding the British record caught by my son Ian, in no way can the poor cod be deemed worth a piece of bait, except of course to become a bait, and an excellent one at that, in its own right. Our record scaled eleven ounces. Two to four ounces is very much nearer the norm. Again, a delicate little fish, even more so than the pouting. Most die immediately of sheer shock when handled, leaving a tell-tale covering of small golden scales in the palm of the hand. Why not then push a 6/0 hook to a steel trace through it before sending it back down; a firm favourite with conger and bass.

Pollack

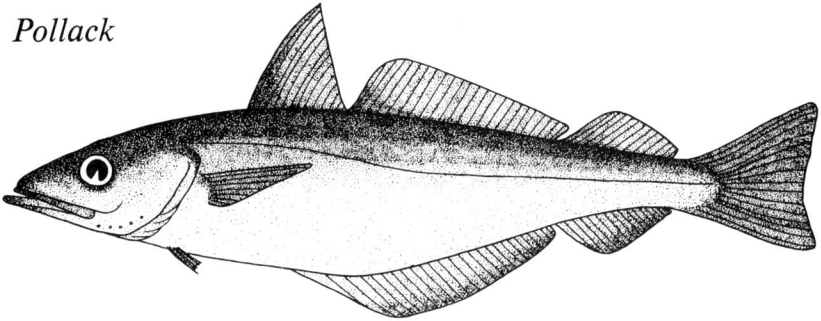

Pollack – Pollachius pollachius: a protruding lower jaw puts it apart from its look alikes. Pollack lack the pectoral spot of the whiting, and light lateral line of the coalfish. Pollack have no chin barbel and a very dark lateral line arched over the pectoral fins. Colouration: dark brown on the upper back, giving way to golden flanks. Shades of colouration are very abrupt.

Wherever there are rocks, invariably pollack will not be too far away. I can think of several instances where the quality of dinghy pollack can rival double figure fish often enjoyed on reefing charters. An odd one might push even as high as 15lbs, but to get beyond the 20lb barrier or threaten the 26lb record, it would have to be a top class wrecking trip.

Closer to shore, much of the best pollack sport is to be had in areas best described as a little dodgy, certainly for the beginner or first time visitor anyway. Rocky outcrops; tide races created by rocky headlands, submerged reefs and rock pinnacles; hardly the best areas to be getting initial dinghy experience. But by the same token, areas not to be missed by those well able to handle their craft after seeking out and taking some local advice on tidal conditions. Good pollack fishing invariably goes hand in glove with tidal disturbance; never the type of situation where total relaxation can be assured. If it is not actual conditions, then the hard fighting antics of a hooked fish will test every resource. In ninety-nine per cent of situations, pollack fishing is best done on the drift. Pollack are one of the elite bunch of fish to have earned themselves a large scale cult following.

Ground coverage is a vital pre-requisite for success. Offerings must be taken to the fish rather than waiting for them to find the boat. Feeding may take place anywhere between the bottom and mid water, so a tactical approach plays a very large part in exploiting the pollack's advanced predatory nature. For this reason, almost all serious pollack fishing is done with artificial lures, quite the most efficient of which are rubber sandeels with the 'swimming' tails. Numerous sizes, colours and designs are currently available, the majority of which follow a basic theme. In deep water, specific colours are unimportant. Most people plump for red. Taken below about thirty feet, the colour red ceases to exist, appearing as black. Completely black imitation eels have accounted for many good fish. No doubt the very lightest colours will be picked out by feeding fish. In shallow water, colour could play a more important role. Alex Ingram started the ball rolling down at Mevagissy; the rest seemed to paddle along in his wake. During the early seventies, his redgills accounted for more specimen and record fish probably than all time before had managed to accumulate. Now the record situation has levelled itself out as more realistic upper limits have been achieved.

Redgills, Eddystone eels and the rest work on the principal of emulating natural movements, ingeniously brought about by the right angled foot at the end of the tail. In deep water, twelve to twenty foot traces are called for, tied to a linked weighted french boom rig known as a flying collar. Dropped to the bottom, line is retrieved steadily. Over a wreck, for example, the height at which fish are feeding can be gauged approximately from the sounder printout giving some indication as to how far up to be bringing the lure. Otherwise, it is guess-work and over really deep water mid water is often enough. However, experiences gained while fishing moderately deep lying reefs in the Scillies have taught me to keep on going until the boom hits the end eye. We had fish making last ditch attacks right on the surface. Stopping mid water would probably have put these fish right off. Keeping the motion going, even with a taking fish is the key to success. Never try to strike a fish. An interested pollack will move in behind a lure, taking and kicking for bottom in one swift move, driving the hook home on itself. Trolling rubber sandeels is a different matter. Movement is given to the lure as the boat keeps underway very slowly. Put plenty of line between lure and boat. Line twisting is a problem with trolling, calling for at least a couple of swivels, plus an anti-kink vane. Weighting is done with long thin, preferably spiral, leads amounts of which will be determined by conditions. This is the technique for shallow reefy ground where fish feed quite close to the surface. Either hold the rod, or have only the last foot poking over the transom. Be sure also and have the drag lightly set, thumbing the spool in order to gain line. Pollack are decidedly not the kind of fish that allow mistakes to go by unpunished.

By virtue of the fact that pollack are often a target for novice charter parties, feathering is a particularly widely used method, proving highly effective with average fish of between 2–5 pounds. What it misses in quality it more than compensates for with quality. In shallow to moderate depths it is at its best, for in the main, feathering only exploits the very lowest levels. However, as pollack have particularly good eyesight, fish seeing the feathers from mid water may be drawn down on to them. I should imagine that everyone including novices knows how to work a set of feathers, so no more on that. Just keep the things on the move and a little way clear of bottom. Not actually hitting bottom shouldn't make one iota of difference to the pollack. What it will do is ensure far fewer hang ups and resultant tackle losses.

Plastic squids, affectionately known as muppets, rigged in similar fashion to feathers on short snoods above the weight, or if you like, a chrome jig, will also take their share of the fish, though experience has shown shallow water pollack to favour only one colour at once, this varying from day to day. Only one or two natural baits can match artificials. Leading the field is a live sandeel worked exactly as if it were a lure. Put a 4/0 hook into the mouth and out through the gills, nicking it into the belly skin. Ragworm is the only remaining natural worthy of particular note. A truly lethal bait capable of putting pollack into a real feeding frenzy – but only for brief periods when, for reasons of reproduction, ragworm take to free swimming in open water. Is it any wonder they drive fish crazy? I suppose it might be feasible for a bit of fun fishing, or in the interests of not over risking things, to put a live prawn, worm or sandeel out under a sliding float at anchor. In calm conditions, drifting along the edge of a headland or outer harbour might be worth while. Certainly free lining sandeel from a drifting boat in flat conditions on summer evenings can prove a useful technique. No weight, just a swivel and hooked sandeel allowed to swim freely; very deadly. Most inshore summer pollack fishing is at its best towards dusk.

Finally, when fishing any craggy area known to expose itself, or worse still, lie dangerously just below the surface, always approach it at low water. That way you see things at their worst, in the knowledge that all the time, water depth is building under the hull, lessening any danger. Not that real dangers should exist. It would, however, be irresponsible not to highlight potential problems and offer suitable advice. Treated with respect, the rewards should more than justify all the homework. Don't be afraid to seek some local advice, and above all else take it literally to the letter.

Coalfish

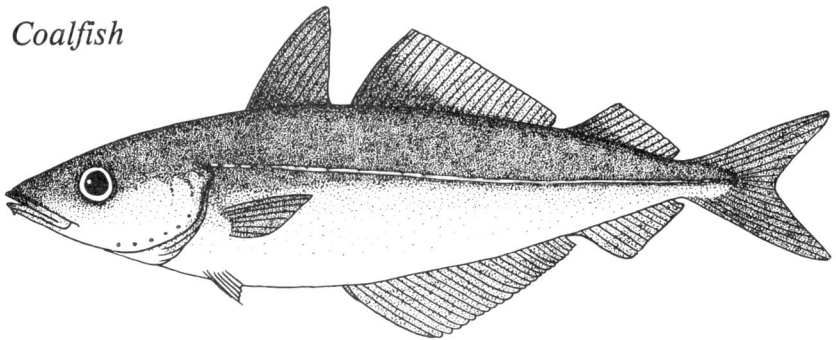

Coalfish – Pollachius virens: lower jaw only marginally longer than upper, with a minute chin barbel. Lateral line is almost straight. Colouration: deep green on back and upper sides with a very prominent white lateral line.

Why nature decided to place two species as similar as pollack and coalfish in the same area of sea has me wondering, not that I'm complaining. Both fight equally hard with the coalfish perhaps having something of an edge in growth potential. Obviously, there will be a reason which probably hinges on the extent of each fish's distribution. Whereas pollack lean towards a southerly nature, though far from absent even in the very north, coalfish distribution works in reverse. We Brits are very fortunate anglers in living geographically at a latitude visited by sub-tropical species as a northerly limit, as well as by sub-arctic fishes using our islands as a southerly limit. The diversity of fishes is, to say the least, vast, a sort of fantastic piscatorial cocktail. We should be more than pleased to be blessed with the fighting qualities of both these game fish in every sense of the word. Why then the query about two similar fish sharing the same niche? Well, it's just our way of saying that much of what has already been written of the tactics required to catch pollack has equal value here.

In the south west, pollack dominate the inshore heavy ground scene, with what coalfish there are content to fatten up further offshore over the well-lardered wrecks. Moving further north towards the Scottish border region sees a different story unfold. Throughout the entire British Isles, overlap is evident. Only the emphasis switches. Inshore, small coalfish form quite large shoals close to kelp and broken ground. Many of those small fish observed weaving in and out of Scottish pier supports are small coalfish. Without any doubt, the best way of catching these fish, usually up to a couple of pounds, is with mackerel feathers. Only in very much deeper water do the bigger fish put in a forceful appearance, which, sadly puts them for the most part outside the dinghy fishing brief, but not completely. Deep sea lochs and sheltered Hebridean bays offer the only regular chance. Those famous gantocks, once the stopping-off point for so many huge cod entering the upper Clyde lochs to spawn, hold a reasonable head of better fish. Perhaps a flying collar rig might pull up a surprise or two.

Haddock

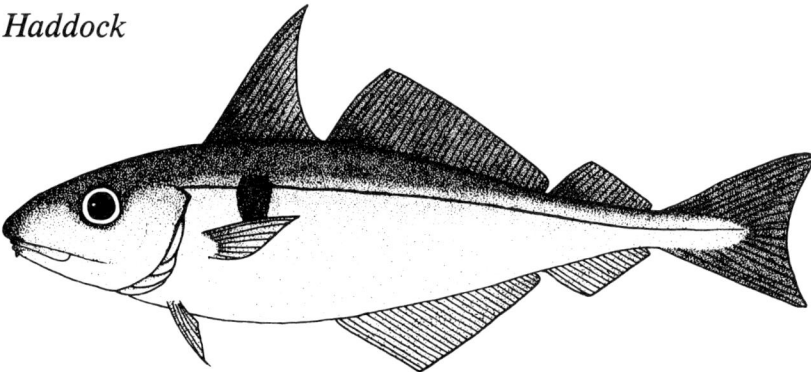

Haddock – Melanogrammus aeglefinus: immediately identified by the apostle's thumb print or dark blotch across the dark lateral line directly above the pectoral fin. Colouration: greenish brown on the upper back, becoming lighter on the flanks and underparts.

Commercial pressures being what they now are, haddock are far from common to rod and line anglers anywhere these days. They were never numerous fish in the first place; more a species prone to setting up small isolated communities here and there, often quite close to shore, well within dinghy range. This has undoubtedly contributed much to their longevity, keeping them tucked out of harm's way. Not that commercials would not want to exploit them; more a case of either not knowing, or being prevented – two factors constantly being challenged. If you drop on a good little hot spot, do not feel obliged to tell everyone about it. Much of the very best haddock fishing these days comes to anglers fishing from small boats.

There was a time when I was well and truly captivated by haddock mania – haddiction, if you'll pardon the pun. My outings were geared around seeing at least a few of the critturs in the fish box. Fortunately, because of their feeding habits, they never came at the expense of other equally acceptable fish like whiting and cod, though to the specialist, haddock can make a number of specific demands. Deep lying muddy ground is the first thing to look for, preferably with a good scattering of queen scallops, other shellfish and brittlestars.

It goes without saying then that soft shellfish baits appeal to a very large number of fish. Scallops, razorfish, mussels, cockles and clams are all successful. Worm baits too will take their toll. I've even had a few grab mackerel strips jigged for coalfish at Shetland. That haddock will go for a fish bait is very interesting. As is true of quite a number of fish, Cornish waters boast the biggest Britain has to offer, despite there not being a great many numerically speaking compared with other places. Cornish catches fall into two categories – accidental and deliberate. The bulk are accidents, picked up on thin mackerel strips put out for fish like whiting out on the sharking grounds. Those taken deliberately are in the main winter fish caught on worm or fish baits close to shore around the edge of the Manacles reef including the current record at 13-11-4. Apparently, as haddock get really big, so their mode of life changes dramatically and the bigger fish become no longer happy in company, turning into loners with a catholic appetite, a fact worthy of a little experimentation in areas known to have a double figure potential. Scotland produces more specimen haddock than most other places combined. A six pound fish is a real beauty; getting one bigger could prove to be extremely difficult.

Despite the many hours I have put in I can see no pointers in favour of either anchoring or drifting as a best bet; both approaches have their days. Selection depends very much on day to day conditions and whether fish have tended to spread themselves about all over the place, as opposed to being tightly grouped. Haddock are not adverse to giving chase to a moving meal, and drifting certainly offers greater ground coverage. Put the anchor down if fish suddenly burst onto the feed. Loch Ryan used to produce agreeable numbers of nice haddock some years ago, until commercial pressure killed sport stone dead without ever exploiting the fish themselves.

Their principal source of food, the queen scallop, was given the treatment instead, forcing the fish on to pastures new. Many of Scotland's other deep water lochs right the way up to the northern Isles harbour a good head of haddock. Even the inner Clyde system produces a few. Brian will sulk long and hard for my saying this, but on one of his early dinghy trailing visits to the Clyde, he returned a boat load of the things, thinking them to be very big pouting. They say the best remembered lessons are the most painful ones! Coming down the north sea coast, haddock are reasonably abundant, although fairly small, as far south as Yorkshire. Sadly, much of the muddy ground lies some way off, and is not always the easiest of areas to negotiate in a small boat at best. Quite the best haddock sport I have been lucky enough to sample came while dinghy fishing the many little sheltered bays of Arran.

Ideas on terminal tie-ups differ greatly. What does not is the action to take when a fish shows interest. My preference is for a french boom just above the weight, with a yard long nylon length to a 2/0 hook. Simple flowing traces work equally well. When the take comes be sure and give it time. These are slow, determined feeders with particularly soft mouths and it is far better to let a taking fish get the hook in deeply. Despite their size, haddock give an excellent account of themselves on light tackle. It soon becomes easy to tell the dogged head-bumping fight of a haddock compared with the laborious pumping required for cod. Unnecessary pressure could result in a light hook-hold tearing free. The same is true when trying to lift a good fish aboard. Always use a landing net. Given a sporting chance the haddock is one of the better fighting fish.

Plaice

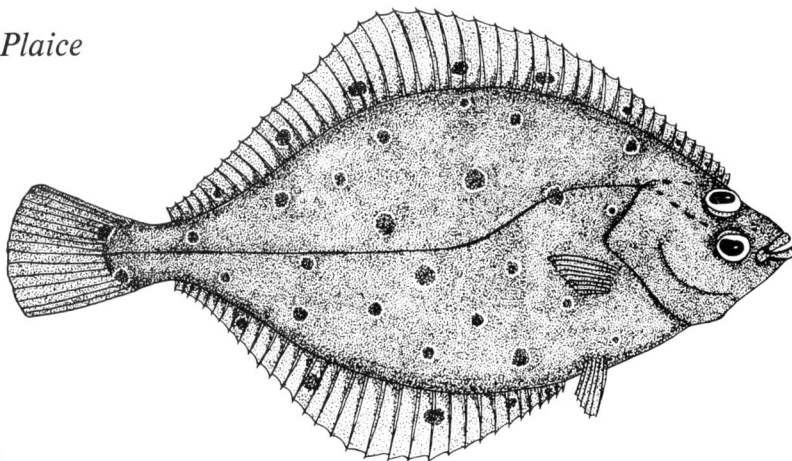

Plaice – Pleuronectes platessa: mouth situated on the right hand side of the eyes. Colouration alone should be enough to identify this flatfish, it being brown on the upper side, with a scattering of red spots. On the under side it is pure pearly white. The fish is smooth all over, with a series of bony bumps between the lateral line and the eyes.

An odd plaice or two picked up here and there is generally accepted by many these days as being something of a welcome bonus. Catch half a dozen and the flags are out. Such reactions have prompted speculation in certain quarters of the press that all is not what it used to be. Fewer and fewer big catch or specimen reports, even from the commercial sector, now have people saying that inshore plaice fishing has irreversibly had its day. To a degree, this is true. Many old and trusted marks have now gone, picked clean by every cowboy able to get his hands on a net. Reactions however are leaning too much towards unfounded alarmism. There are still plenty of plaice marks, for the most part waiting the arrival of some pioneering dinghy, as well as others whose location is kept under wraps. Simply, the rules governing getting the best from plaice have changed. No longer is it a case of trailing drifted baits along any bit of clean seabed and popping the anchor over when a few are found. Rocks, scars, bits of reefs and similar underwater obstructions lie at the heart of today's best plaice potential. Yes, exactly the kind of stuff anglers of old would have steered well clear of. Tucked in amongst many such areas of net resistant ground lie smatterings of food-rich sand, and the shallower the water the less likely the possibility of unwanted tampering. These are the sanctuaries now of the inshore summer plaice. Where we fish, heavy scars intersect a very large expanse of shallow-lying sand. From depths of only four feet at low water, catches topping 500 fish, and individuals bettering 5 pounds have been recorded. Plaice of between 5 and 7 pounds are reported with some frequency from banks like the Skerries, though I feel the 10-3-8 record will remain supreme for quite a long time. I suspect 1½ to 2lbs is nearer the average.

Catching plaice is never a difficult pursuit, but finding them can be a problem. Treat yourself to an inshore chart and a few days' experimentation. And should you find the fish, I for one won't object if you never say a word to anyone. Plaice are amongst the first fish to depart the backend inshore scene, returning again in the spring, spent, thin and weary, victims of the rigours of seeding future generations well offshore. It takes weeks of concentrated feeding to restretch that skin with firm prime flesh, so they are hardly worth catching until the summer gets into full swing. Fortunately, a comprehensive opportunist diet makes for a quick recovery. Everything from worms and shellfish to sandeels get the hungry eye. But often, particular marks offer rather singular feeding, which may in turn lead to pre-occupation. This tends mainly to happen over inshore mussel beds where tiny seed mussels are the prime target. As bait, large shelled mussels are equally acceptable. Anything else may well be refused.

When thinking about terminal gear suitable to present baits to their best advantage, mark size and bed structure must be considered too. At anchor, two boomed metal paternosters are at their most efficient. Any bottom dapping rig will catch, including french or plastic booms, multi hook flowing traces or simple nylon paternosters, but only a metal pat can both spread

Another fine brace on a paternoster.

and work a number of baits at the same level effectively. Hooks need to be size 1 to 1/0 and, where possible, long shanked.

Plaice are exceedingly greedy creatures, prone to gulping baits down at high speed. In our experience, less than ten in a hundred end up lip hooked when they are feeding heavily. That small mouth was not designed to accommodate deep disgorging fingers, which is a great pity really, as so many of the smaller fish go back far less than one hundred per cent well. At least with a long hook shank you are in with a chance of something showing to get hold of. A pair of long nosed pliers will aid surgery. Plaice can be an excellent fighting fish on suitable tackle, so don't overwhelm them with gear capable of bullying a tope.

To anchor or to drift – that is the question? Answering it is far from clear-cut. Certainly, fishing at rest accounts for big catches, but only when good concentrations of fish are to hand. Where plaice are generally widespread, baits are better taken in search of them. If so, go for a longer hook length to keep the bait at an effective level. Plaice will swim up and take a bait coming in slightly overhead. Most would much rather give chase to a bait bobbling along at eye level. Where strong tides or stiff breezes create rapid boat movement, long flowing traces work best. Personally, I pin all my faith in lugworm on the hook, followed closely by rag. However, on the Skerries bank, which incidentally could be fished by a fast dinghy from Dartmouth on a fine day, anglers have learned to cope with some of the worst tidal conditions imaginable, taking big early season fish on a wide variety of

A plump specimen plaice sorted out from the run-of-the-mill with blacklug.

baits. Traces of up to twenty feet are used. Shoals of big fat sandeels get washed over the banks, picked off by all manner of fish lying just over the down tide slopes in ambush. Long sandeel fillets and thin squid strips fish well. Cocktails incorporating worm, shellfish and peeler crab also give great success. Remember, when leaving long strips of fluttering bait free of the hook, not to strike until you are sure the hook has been taken well inside the mouth.

As hinted earlier, we know for a fact that good plaice catches are still being made and, despite what others might suggest, big plaice also exist. One of the major problems in getting to grips with specimens is often a profusion of smaller fish. Always first off the mark when a bait goes down, they don't give better fish any real chance. To catch big plaice, either these smaller fish must be deterred, or the baits be taken elsewhere to where bait robbers are fewer. Unfortunately, in the early stages of a day's sport, it is not always easy to ascertain just how things are going to go. Plaice feeding often follows the pattern of a chain reaction. During the early stages, a few tugs and pulls might result in a mere handful of fish, but plaice are naturally hyper-inquisitive, so let this be their downfall. Those first few on the scene draw in more, and in turn still more as the hours tick by. By the end of the session, fish are fighting to jump the suicide queue, which is when you inconveniently run out of bait. The only thing liable to deter them is nightfall. I cannot recall ever having taken plaice after dark. Now, to alleviate bait shortages, we take along a few packs of the previous winter's left-over frozen blacklug. We were reluctant to try it at first, but when eventually we did, it rapidly cut down the numbers of smaller fish. Big plaice showed little hesitation, so perhaps this is one way of coaxing the better fish. First get masses of them interested with fresh blowlug, then swop it for something attractive only to the bigger fish.

Dab

When first we start sea fishing, all things flat get labelled as plaice. If the truth were known, most would turn out to be dabs. Very widespread fish, not unlike plaice, dabs are more obliging and on average smaller. At times, little 'postage stamps' even have a nuisance value. Otherwise inshore dabs command much respect. Present in coastal waters all year round, a mile or two offshore they can be quite numerous throughout the summer, hitting both their numerical, as well as conditional peak towards the onset of winter. Cold weather does much to sharpen dabs' appetites bringing them very close to the low water mark. Over clean ground especially, they make easy pickings. Other types of sea bed that can attract include stones scattered over sand, with small pockets and individuals even setting up home on tiny smatters of sand, right in amongst heavy, bouldery terrain.

The dab is a fish with quite a wide ranging appetite, willing to tackle just about anything capable of going onto a hook, providing the size is right.

Dab

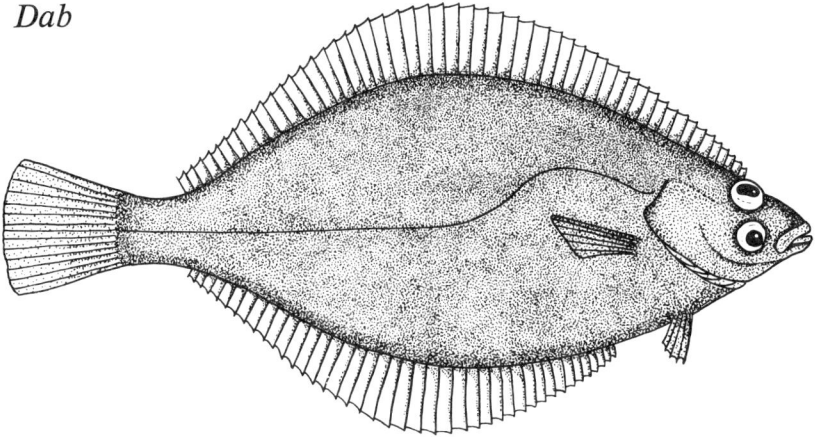

Dab – Limanda limanda: like the plaice, its eyes lie to the left of the mouth. Occasionally, small flecks might suggest its identity to be that of a plaice. Look for a strongly curved lateral line and rough feel when rubbed from tail to head. Colouration: some shade of brown, varying with sea bed conditions.

Though it is not generally realized, small fish strips are appreciated. Shellfish, squid, sandeel strip, crab and more especially worms, put most fish into the box. I have even caught them on bits of barbequed chicken skin when the bait situation has been desperate. One other point worth bearing in mind: baits need not be especially fresh; far from it in fact. Blow lug that has started turning, or is already watery, can drive them wilder than healthy stuff. Too long frozen blacklug only fit for dumping is another great catcher; why then waste decent worm bait? That rancid smell provokes an unbelievable response.

Dabs feed very much as plaice do, taking food either on, or very close to the bottom, bursting from a covering of sand to seize whatever tit-bit comes their way. For just that reason, then, metal paternosters account for big catches by virtue of their ability to work more than one bait at the correct feeding level. A multi-hook flowing trace rig, french booms and similar bottom-exploiting tie-ups all catch dabs. It's a question of just how successful you want to be. Metal paternosters were created with just this sort of work in mind, and this is one instance of modern technology being unable to outdo the rather cruder-looking methods of old. Fortunately, dab feeding habits lend themselves to consistent lip hooking, allowing for meaningful conversation for all but the very best fish. Invariably, dabs hit surface white side up for some reason. Hardly a sporting fish, but without them inshore fishing would suffer a painful blow. Fish of between ½ and ¾ of a pound are probably average and anything topping a pound is a good one. The current record stands at 2-12-4.

Flounder

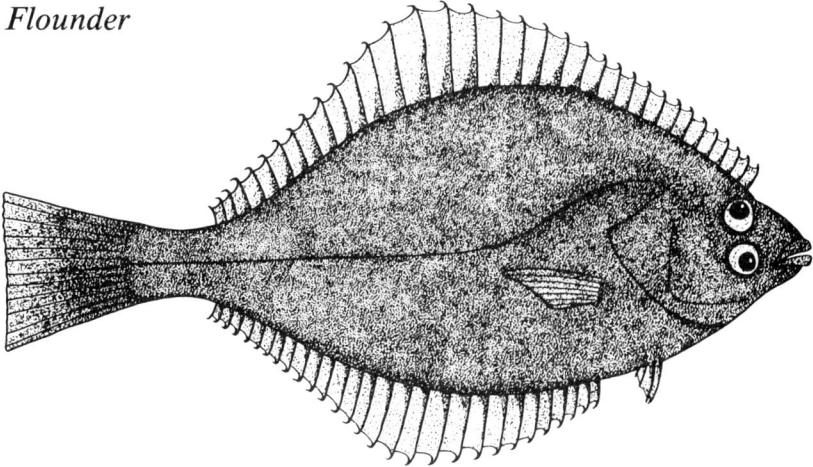

Flounder – Platichthys flesus: again, the eyes are to the left of the mouth. Flounders lack both the rough feel of the dab, and smoothness of the plaice. Instead, they have a scattering of prickles along the lateral line, dorsal and anal base. Colouration: dull greenish brown, possibly with some small pale flecks. The underparts are especially pearly white.

Basically, flounders are a shore angler's fish. There are, however, both times and circumstances under which they do come under scrutiny from small boat owners. The flounder is a fish more fond of saltings, estuarine creeks, inlets and harbours than open sea; anywhere in fact where freshwater influences the salt balance, although they will also frequently tolerate pure salt water. A vital part of their life cycle takes place well offshore towards the end of winter, when mature fish desert traditional haunts to spawn. In late spring, the forerunners arrive back inshore as spent, thin-looking fish which could do well without the strain of being caught. From then until early autumn, most prefer to lurk just beyond shore casting range. In stormy weather when small boats need to search out sheltered water, harbours and inlets often offer the only refuge short of staying at home. This is when flounder fishing and dinghy work can come together with fair rewards.

Dropping shallow water temperatures linked to a need for building reserves of body weight does eventually coax the summer fish right inshore, until large volumes of melted snow water flooding the rivers pushes them back out, after which few mature fish bother to move in again until their spawning is complete. During the inshore push, much of the potential is lost to dinghy rods. Exceptions are areas with vast enclosed expanses of sheltered water like Christchurch, Poole, the Solent inlets and Fowey. Only small boats can hope to even scratch at those potentials. In fact, at Fowey, dinghy anglers have a monopoly on the very best flounder fishing on offer, anywhere. The current record of 5-11-8 is a Fowey fish, and considering the scrap put up by the average fish of 2lbs and under on suitable gear, what sport it must have been.

In common with similar flatties, flounders present no real difficulty in the catching. Try not to make the mistake of hunting out water with too much depth. Flounders will all but crawl up onto the damp sand. Get tucked in close and cast in even closer when conditions dictate. The best fishing comes around the low water period with the fish squeezed into concentrations itching to get back onto the food beds with the first push of the new flood tide. As ever, paternosters are highly effective. But because of the often very shallow nature of productive winter marks, multi-hooked flowing traces could well prove even better with hook sizes 1 to 1/0. Always popular, worm baits probably pick up more flounders than all other baits combined, and bunches of tiny harbour rag are especially favoured. This doesn't necessarily mean worm baits are best; just that they are more popular with anglers. Crab is without equal as the premier flounder bait, especially portions cotton-tied to the hook, or peeled legs slipped up the shank like small worms. Live shrimp fished around commercial shrimp boats catch-riddling at their mooring sometimes provides an interesting alternative.

There is a technique widely used these days with many species of fish, but originally designed primarily with flounder fishing in mind; this is spooning. Modern spoons rely on blade rotation to stimulate fish like cod into further inspecting a bait dangling in open water. With flounders, a flowing trace rig is required. Chromed metal or white plastic spoons both work well, fixed a little way in front of the bait. Kept on the move either from an anchored or slowly drifting boat, spoon rotation stirs up a little 'dust' trail in the mud. The theory is that inquisitive fish follow up the trail, thinking the flashing spoon to be another small flattie trying to make off with a meal too big to handle. Just how a hungry flounder views the situation is a matter of opinion.

Sole

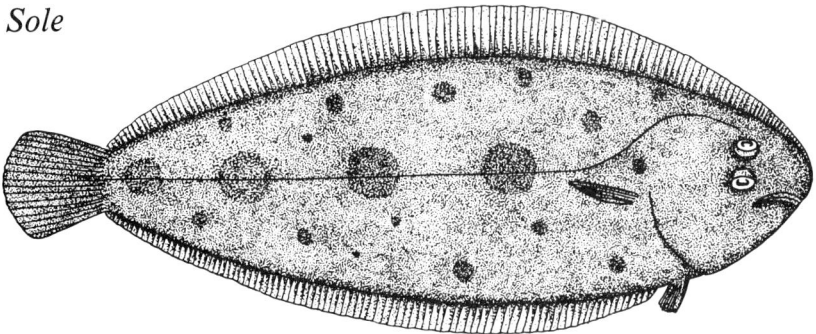

Sole – Solea solea: a long eliptical shape flatfish with a decidedly rough feel. Colouration: a deep uniform greyish brown with irregular darker blotches. There is a conspicuous black spot on the pectoral fin.

Quite a common, widespread inshore fish around much of Britain, but not easy to catch. Knowledge of their presence can mean little without the right approach. Clearly then a specialist fish, exploited more from the shore than from boats. A good tactic could be to listen out for shore reports, then look at the prospect of putting a small boat in from the beach, for the fact is that in a number of areas, small boats offer the best and at times the only access to these fish. Sadly, the number of times dinghies end up on top of the things bears little resemblance to numbers actually caught. Inappropriate tactics lie at the crux of the problem. Approached skilfully, soles are far from hook-shy. Three factors in the main keep catches low. Firstly, hook sizes must be small enough – say 2 to 4 – to get inside that tiny mouth. Secondly, most soles lie dormant during daylight hours, preferring to feed nocturnally. And finally, though fish can be found in waters of differing depths, most prefer it so shallow at times that even a novice shorecaster could conceivably put a bait out too far. Where dinghies have it made is in areas like the Solent, banked along much of the mainland side by marshland, river inlets and muddy creeks; perfect boat sole territory with access to spots where anglers on foot might rarely stray. Try anchoring in one of those creeks at nightfall and be prepared to sit it out until dawn. Small pieces of lug, and to a lesser extent, rag, flicked into the shallows should show a result. Don't expect to fill a box with the things; to catch a couple is good going and anything more is a bonus. Some of the specimens I have seen down there constitute a bonus on their own, with three pounders not uncommon. The British record of 3-12-4 is a nearby Isle of Wight fish.

Over the years I have fished for soles in many corners of the country, but without much success, mainly because trips were either arranged for other species, sole fishing being an afterthought, or because fleeting visits to far-flung places are always potentially adventurous because you have no prior knowledge of what to expect. With the main baits out, little bits of worm would be put over, more in hope than expectation. The amazing thing to come out of this is the tally of excellent other species caught. At Bradwell, for example, I had a good thornback move in through a line of peeler crab and herring baits, to pick up a half inch portion of ragworm. In the Solent, stingrays and smoothhounds did the same. Elsewhere, big lesser spotted dogs, bull huss and even conger have given their intended baits the cold shoulder. Could it be that, like people, fish can also get a bit bored with eating big meals, preferring a tit-bit instead? Whatever the reason, be on your guard for this when sole fishing. Tie the trace out of 30lb breaking strain mono, giving yourself a fighting chance; after dark it certainly won't deter the soles.

Turbot

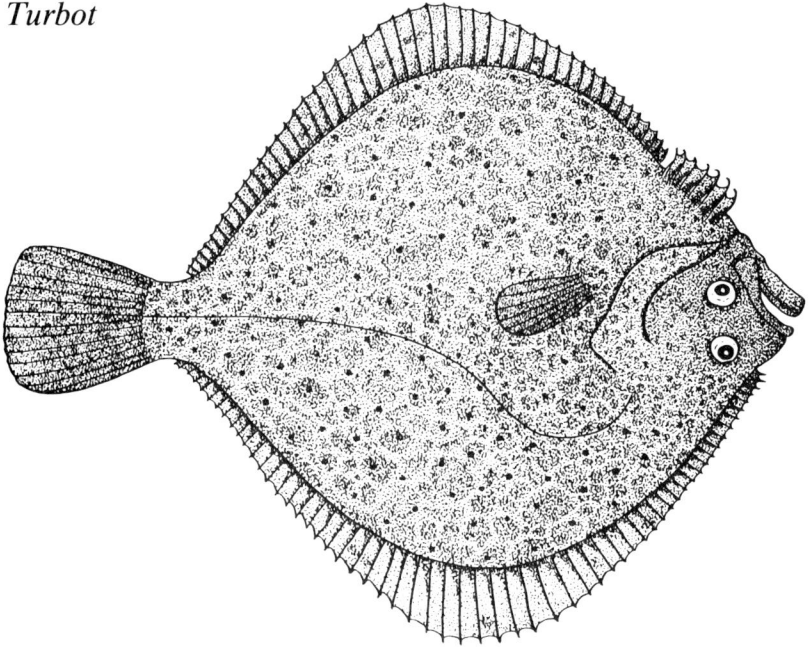

Turbot – Scophthalmus maximus: a noticeably round-looking fish. Unlike plaice and the like, turbot have eyes to the right of the mouth which on the drawing makes it look upside down. The entire upper surface is covered with hard bony tubercles. Colouration: can vary greatly to blend with differing sea-bed structures. Flecks, blotches and mottling feature well in each disguise.

The turbot is the ultimate flatfish prize, but is not exactly a regular small boat proposition. Few indeed are the holding areas accessible by dinghy, yet I have seen some impressive specimens come ashore from boats under sixteen feet. Coverack in Cornwall was once famed for its inshore turbot fishing, and the Channel Islanders, too, get a reasonable share. Even the Skerries and marks out in Lannacombe Bay off the Devon coast could be reached with a sturdy small boat on the right day. Otherwise, an odd turbot could turn up anywhere over clean or shingly ground. Reports of more than one should signal the initiation of a little investigative homework. What we are looking for are areas of greater than normal tidal activity, such as caused by banks suddenly surging up out of deep water, creating a great scouring flush of water across their tops. Predatory fish are well aware that in conditions such as these, small food fishes like sandeels, unless they seek refuge by going to ground, are at the mercy of the current. Hungry fish like turbot lie on the down tide slopes of gullies, dips and even the bank edges in wait. As dinner is delivered to them by the tide, all they need do is spring up, picking off their unsuspecting victims as they are swept overhead.

On well-formed banks, turbot fishing is best done on the drift. Very long flowing traces, sometimes as much as twenty feet, carry sandeels or long thin belly cuts of mackerel on 2/0 to 4/0 hooks. It is helpful to pick out a suitable-looking ambush point on the echo sounder, continually drifting over it. Failing this, long, rather more general drifts can be undertaken. With these in mind, it pays to have out plenty of line to compensate for and keep in contact with fluctuating bottom levels. On smaller, less clearly defined marks anchoring might offer some chance of a fish. It is far better where possible to be taking baits to the fish rather than living in the hope of one leaving its ambush position, though undoubtedly at certain times this is just what they do. The one bonus to come out of all this is the appeal this approach is going to have to other fishes like rays, brill, and bass. Even in the absence of the intended target, days will not be dull.

All round the country little pockets of small to middle range fish in the 3 to 10lb bracket have been known to exist. One I can bring to mind lies to the west of Scotland's Coreswall light, another very much nearer to Loch Ryan itself. Periodically, a big flattie latches onto a tope or thornback bait, and occasionally these have topped the magical twenty pound mark. It is under circumstances such as these that local dinghy owners could explore the situation more fully, while at the same time continue their normal course of fishing. As turbot are so actively predatory by nature, baits with natural movement as opposed to static fish lumps will stimulate the feeding more readily. What I would suggest here is swopping that flowing trace for a four to six foot length tied to a french boom fixed a foot or so above the weight. In essence, the bait would still be working bottom. What the french boom would do is induce a more natural fluttering movement to the sandeel or long mackerel cut as it is picked up by the tide. Most of the accidental Scottish turbot I have seen fell to baits just clear of bottom. In fact, one twenty pounder took right on the surface having followed a small pouting up.

Brill

Despite its being a very much less common rod-caught fish than the turbot, brill are in fact more widespread, certainly on the middle range trawling grounds, suggesting perhaps little more than a dislike of the shallower inshore grounds more used to angling attention. Otherwise, what has been said of the catching of turbot is equally true here. With the possible exception of the Channel Islands, Alderney in particular, I should think that all other small boat specimens are accidentally caught. Some numbers are taken from Skerries and around Lannacombe Bay. Despite their not being a common inshore fish, we felt it worthwhile including a fleeting mention here due to their many similarities to the turbot. A ten pound turbot, though a fabulous fish, is nothing to go writing to the press about, but a ten pound brill is a monster with 4–8lbs nearer the norm, so bear this in mind and be sure no confusion exists. Feel the back of all big flatties, whose eyes lie to the right

Brill

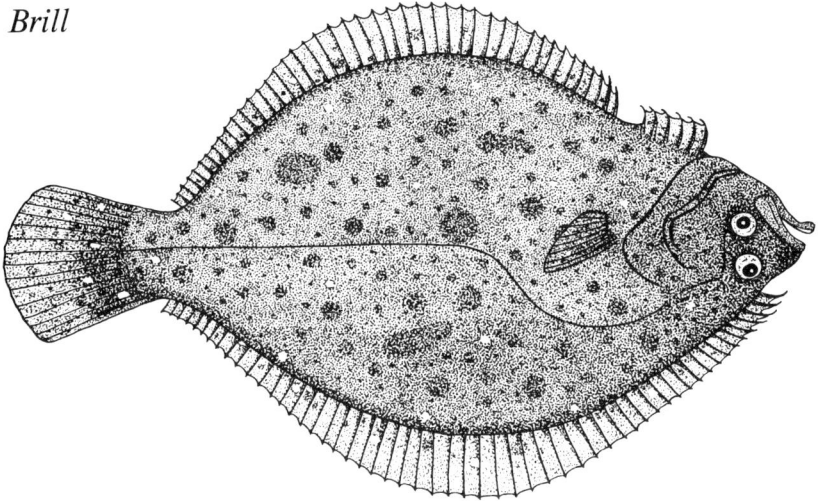

Brill – Scophthalmus rhombus: similar to, but less round than, the turbot. It too has eyes to the right of the mouth. Separating turbot from brill is done by looking for no bony tubercles over the upper back so obvious with turbot. Colouration: again variable, with blotches, spots and flecks over some shade of brown.

of their mouth; a scattering of hard bony lumps means turbot, and anything else deserves much closer investigation, as more likely than not it will be a brill.

Tope

So far as regular dinghy fishing goes, tope represent the ultimate test. Perhaps not everyone would agree, some seeing them as just too much of a handful for such confined spaces. Who am I to argue? Everyone must know their own, the boats, and their crew's capabilities.

All I will say is that I cannot get enough of them. Brian is less enthusiastic, once being floored and almost capsized by a 30 pounder in a thirteen foot boat. I must agree that having had more than a few 'unforgettable moments', I would prefer not to be fishing from much less than a sixteen footer. Otherwise, tope offer fantastic fun. For the most part, they swim close inshore as the summer warms up, particularly during settled weather. In Scotland things begin a little later, lasting into the early winter. The general 'stock fish' are run-of-the-mill males, often of good average size, but rarely fish of a lifetime. If you have been pestered in late summer by hoards of bait-robbing mini-tope up to a couple of pounds, then feel heartened, because only into recognised nursery areas do big females venture in the early summer, long before the main run, to drop their pups. Clean to scrubby, stony ground is favoured. However, never on any account rule out rocky, even reefy areas. We have a mate, Micky Mairs, with a

Tope

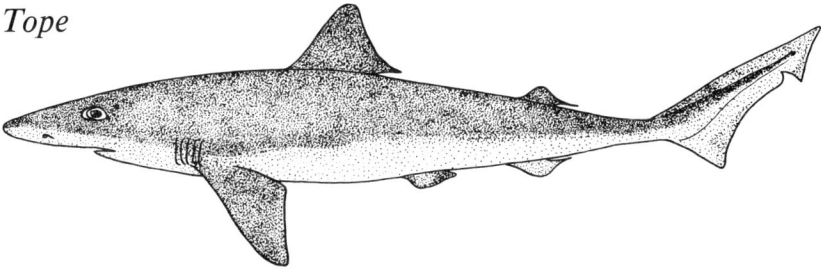

Tope – Galeorhinus galeus: typically shark-like in every detail. Unlike its near relatives, it possesses no spines, spots or weak crushing teeth, its teeth being relatively big, pointed and sharp. Colouration: uniformly greyish to greyish brown.

passion for heavy ground summer codding. Paternostered soft backed crab is the bait he uses, and the number of big tope he ends up catching is unbelievable. He hates the things, yet can't get away from them! Mackerel are what supposedly draw a lot of predators inshore. Where we live this is not so. Our tope do feed readily on mackerel given the chance, it being the number one bait, but by the time they arrive on the scene, much of the best toping is over with. Tope, like many fish, are opportunist feeders, making the most of whatever is locally abundant. Before the mackerel arrive, flatties, whiting and pout provide provide the staple diet. This situation forces us either to baiting with small bottom fish, or using frozen mackerel. We have caught some exceptional fish on frozen bait.

For the most part, tope fishing is conducted on the bottom. Nothing does this better than a simple flowing trace. Experience has shown that in some areas, tope go more readily for baits on nylon traces than with steel, a case of more takes, but less fish due to bite-offs. As a compromise, a couple of yards of 100 pound nylon tied to six inches of heavy braided steel and a 10/0 hook catches all the fish we want. Steel to beat the teeth, backed by strong mono to minimise breakages due to line abrasion caused by the tope's rough-skinned tail. Bait size seems to make little difference with feeding fish. Like many people, I used to read and digest long rambling accounts in the magazines about bait variations to suit particular moods. Make a bait neat, fluttering and attractive by all means; at times of shortages, one fillet split lengthways makes two good baits. At times of acute shortages, quarter fillets, or even thin strips, have all caught fish. I tend to let everyone else grab all the fillet cuts. Far and away the best bait I find is the head and guts, hooked through the eye socket. I've had as many as three fish come to one baited hook. On the other side of the coin, young Ian used to get the job of paternostering for whiting as a fallback bait. Tope to 17lbs have picked up the tiny mackerel scraps. Trot the big baits down tide, set the drag on mid tension, knock the reel out of gear, set the ratchet and wait. Mackerel allowing, put out a rubby dubby bag. Then sit back and relax, using the ratchet as an alarm.

Stage one – guiding a tope into position ready for tailing.

A text book tope take starts with a long screaming run, followed by a pause to get the meal into the eating position, then a slower trickle as the food is being dealt with. In theory, then is the time to throw the reel back into gear, locking the spool with the thumb until the hook is driven home; temporarily maintaining thumb tension, adjust the drag to pressurize the fish without parting the line. Any additional tension needed to gain line during pumping should again come from the thumb. Some tope however are non-conformist when it comes to picking up a bait. I've had some take off like marathon sprinters, whilst others react like lethargic pigs with barely the energy to stumble along more than a couple of yards. An odd one might even bite like a whiting. Only experience can indicate how to react to each individual situation; the written word can do little to advise. Trial and error, with some unfortunate never-to-be-repeated mistakes is the way we all have to learn. While all of this is going on, get your crew-mate to bring in the other lines, and along with everything else under the feet, stow them carefully up front. When the trace swivel shows, whoever is going to bring the thing aboard should be gloved and on his knees – praying if it is his first attempt. Take the trace, but never wrap it around the hand, guiding the fish to within grabbing range. Try if possible for the tail, but failing this, pectoral and dorsal fins make good holding points. Grab what you can and in the heaving confusion, thrashing and soaking spray, keep hold. This method of boating avoids the use of gaffs which understandably cause unnecessary damage. I once had a 50 pounder tangled in another line come towards me teeth first. There was nothing else to do but make the best of things. I grabbed it by the throat in a firm strangle-hold. It rocked momentarily on the gunwhale, looking as if it could slide in either direction, then in it came, up-ending me. We all had to stand on the seat until it calmed down. When finally back in the water, it circled the boat a couple of times, glaring, before sinking slowly out of sight.

Some while after, I took out a first-timer keen to have a crack. Ian was first into action with a fish that to all intents was going to be small. Only when it hit the boat on the crest of a wave was its size appreciated. In it came, de-skinning my bare forearm in the process. The idea is to maintain a firm grip of the tail while somebody works up front on freeing the hook. Not with this one though; despite calls for assistance, I was struggling alone. Ian and the other chap had shot up front so far and so fast that when they later emerged, matey had a pointed head. Thirty-four pounds of none-too-partial muscle was going berserk all over the boat, attacking and damaging two rod butts. Now I think twice about boating all but the very best fish for weighing, then release. It has been suggested that the lifting of all sharks from their naturally supportive environment causes the weight of some internal organs to sever small blood vessels, leaving what on the face of things looks like a healthy fish to die slowly. Conservation has long been a part of tope fishing. Let careful handling now do as much for their future well-being, then perhaps with luck the long-standing record of 74-11-0 taken by Ack Harries back in 1964 will again be threatened.

Stage two – a firm grip of both dorsal and tail, teeth gritted, and in she comes.

Starry Smoothhound

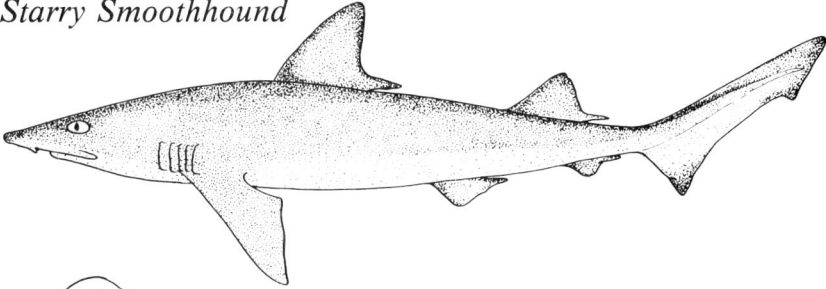

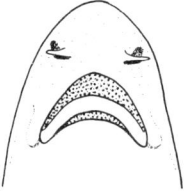

Smoothhounds – Mustelus mustelus and Mustelus asterias: often confused with tope which it superficially resembles. Mouth not typically shark-like, but designed for crushing hard shells with short powerful teeth running along both lips not unlike those of the thornback ray. Colouration: dull grey becoming lighter underneath. Both species are for the most part identical. Mustelus asterias has a scattering of white spots on the back and sides, hence the name starry smoothhound.

My first ever encounter with this power-packed never-say-die fighter came out from Bradwell under the guidance of John Rawle. When eventually I guided a 7 pounder to the waiting net, he smacked it on the back of the head sending the thing back off at break-neck pace. 'What ya do that for?' I asked. 'Well, you looked to be enjoying it so much, I thought you'd like another go', came his reply. Just a pity they don't grow as big as the rest of the shark clan. On the face of things, a sluggish bottom-loving fish not far removed from an average spurdog. Why such a turn of speed is necessary for a fish happy to mooch around the sea bed exercising its powerful ray-like jaws on hard shelled crustaceans isn't really clear. Bob Cox described it as God's gift to sea anglers. Crabs are hardly super-mobile, particularly hermits, the distribution of which goes hand in glove with the presence of smoothhounds during the summer months. With this in mind, take along a fish baited drop net. Threaded onto a 2/0 to 4/0 hook, its point coming out between the main claws, hermits offer the greatest chance of success. Tactically speaking, a simple yard long 40lb nylon flowing trace presents the bait to its best advantage. Failing a supply of hermits, ordinary soft backs and peelers, or at a pinch ragworm, make useful alternatives. Somewhat localised in distribution, parts of Anglesey, the Welsh Bristol Channel coast, bits of north Cornwall, the Solent, and the southern North Sea/English Channel intersection offer the main hope, but be careful not to mistake the fish for a small tope.

Smoothhounds do feed by day. This said, close inshore, more are caught after dark. Clean to muddy, often estuarine, areas attract them. Shallow lying offshore banks offer another source. Night sessions in very shallow water are especially memorable. With only one plane in which to travel, long range hard fought battles are assured. Fishing at anchor close in off the Hampshire shore of the Solent has given me some tremendous sport. I was first shown the ropes by nocturnal fanatic, Dink LeMoignan, around Sowley. A sudden piercing whine from the reel would shake everybody back to life. How fish under ten pounds can manage to take line from a reel under near maximum drag is beyond belief. Eventually, picked out by a torch beam, they would come seemingly beaten to the boat, then off again behind you under the hull. One in particular sticks in my mind. A loud scream of the ratchet, followed by a sudden nothing. Go on, we all said, have another go, little knowing it still had the bait, having doubled back towards the boat. Thinking the bait to be gone, I began winding in only to find it had gone under the other lines, and had missed the prop and drop net, finally coming to rest around the anchor rope. Dink climbed onto the cuddy and started drawing the rope. In the torch light, my other hook could be seen dangling. Dink leaned out hanging from the grab handle to free the hook. Without any warning, inches away from his fingers, all hell let loose. Poor Dink nearly died of shock. Incredibly, it pulled the other hook free, took the same route back, avoiding all the obstacles, and was brought to the net some time later at 10¼ pounds. Some of the fish that night topped 15 pounds; what wouldn't I give to catch a 20 pounder, the current record standing at 28lbs, the same weight in fact as the other smoothhound record. An eerie sight in the torch beam, those big, cold staring eyes piercing right through you.

Smoothhound

Only a smattering of small white spots separates Mustelus mustelus from the already detailed Mustelus asterias. From an angling view point, everything else is the same. At one time, mustelus was more common in some areas than asterias. More recent times have seen something of a reversal of this role. In fact, I have only ever seen one mustelus caught, taken by Dink LeMoignan from the western Solent. As both are a match for one another this point is purely academic.

Spurdog

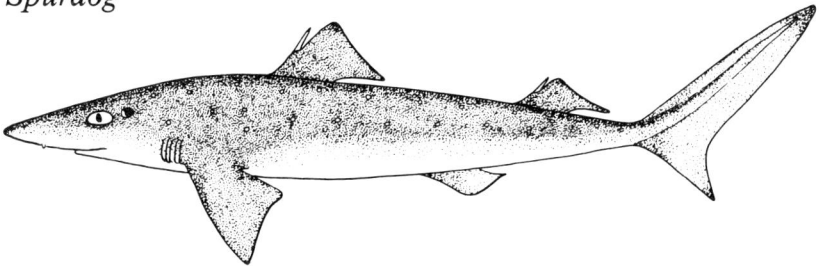

Spurdog – Squalus acanthias: typically shark-like in general body shape. Easily distinguished from similar fish by a single prominent spine in front of both dorsal fins. Colouration: grey with white spots along back and sides.

A very important, even popular fish for the offshore scene. Without the visiting spurdog packs, many boat anglers would struggle for fish of reasonable weight. Being relatively deep water fish, dinghy anglers tend only to scratch at the periphery. Early summer marks the beginning of the invasion.

Unlike the two spotted dogs, these are gregarious, shoaling fish. Find one and you could be in for a bonanza. Moreover, shoals usually consist of a single sex, all of very similar size. There is no real saying what this might be, though in the main most shoals cover the eight to twelve pound range and are more often than not females. A 16lb spurdog is a real specimen with the record currently standing at 21-3-7. A great pity, really, as many of the first early catches end up giving birth to dozens of yolk sac pups all over the bottom of the boat, which doesn't do anyone any good. As the season progresses, so the problem recedes. All in all a very widespread fish, common around much of the British Isles. Wales receives a pretty healthy measure, as does south west Scotland, parts of Cumbria, the Isle of Wight and much of the eastern channel.

Spurdog seem less in need of their food on the bottom than other dogfishes. Lures as well as baits can score, and I have had many on jigged, baited mackerel feathers. In the interests of knocking up a big weight, competition fishermen attack them with strong multi-hook rigs. Heavy nylon is adequate, providing a careful watch is kept for over-chaffing close to the hook. It is far more sporting, though, to approach any fish with a single bait and tackle balanced to maximise the measure of its fight. Actually, spurdog give a reasonable account of themselves. Being specific, I prefer a french boom rig with a fish bait just dapping bottom. Their eyesight seems to play as important a part as their keen sense of smell. This rig helps exploit both facets. One odd thing I have noticed is an apparent sense of loyalty. One fish on its journey boatward may well be flanked by a number of its mates. Probably, loyalty is an overstatement. Certainly this is not a rare event. Not as agile a fish as the spotty dogs, spurs present little threat of skin abrasions. Instead, a vicious-looking spine lies to the fore of each dorsal fin. Keep the fish for eating by all means, but be sure and kill it first as a safety precaution. One other point worthy of note, never gut spurdog over the side while fishing is still in progress, as it can scatter the rest of them far and wide.

Lesser Spotted Dogfish

Much maligned and frequently abused, the single word best able to sum up this abundant, ever-hungry little shark is 'inevitable'! Out there somewhere is one swimming round with your name on its back. To a degree, anti-dogfish agitation is understandable. After all, when time and bait are at a premium in the pursuit of better things, the last straw has to be the insignificant hanging around in plague proportions. This of course does not apply to everyone. None-the-less, a lot of anglers seem willing to jump onto the anti-doggie band wagon. Rare indeed are those with any sort of a kind

Lesser Spotted Dogfish

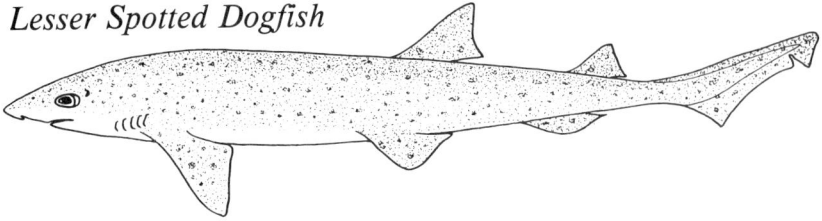

Lesser Spotted Dogfish – Scyliorhinus canicula: a very rough skinned fish, similar at a glance to the larger bull huss. Positioning of the fins is one way of telling the two apart. But by far the easiest at a glance difference to spot is the positioning of the nasal flaps in relation to the mouth. These almost join in the middle and overlap the front of the mouth.

word on the subject. Beaten, unnecessarily killed and generally abused, small dogfish now seem to have developed an hereditary persecution complex. Try raising a stick over the head of one and watch it cringe and close its eyes ready for the impact. Some of the treatment handed out is totally uncalled for. One anonymous journalist used to slit them from vent to eyeball, drag his hook free, then laugh as they swam away. With so many out there, and incidentally a good proportion in the 2-3lb bracket, nothing short of genocide would minimise their nuisance potential. The only time they tend to lose their bad name is when one pushes the 4-1-13 record.

While almost any bait presented in any way close to the bottom will draw a response, for those actually wanting the things, a flowing trace or french boom rig carrying a fish-baited 4/0 to strong nylon trace is the approach. Dogfish teeth are not exactly designed for cutting. Instead, they wear away progressively at monofilament until eventually it parts. This could take several fish, so keep an eye on the line adjacent to the hook, effecting a re-tie when necessary. Sod's Law dicatates that doomed traces only actually part when bringing in something special, never with mere dogfish chomping at the bit. I would say mackerel and herring strips catch most dogfish, followed by worms, soft crab and squid. Only when moving into the shellfish arena does interference taper off, with mussels apparently having one of the greatest deterrent effects. Otherwise, great swarms of the things pester their way into shallow sandy, stony areas, staying put until late autumn, perhaps even longer in deeper water. From Shetland to the Scillies, east and west, they abound. One word of caution about handling the things: invariably, they manage to wrap their tails around the back of your hand during disgorging. Probably reaction to having the hook wrenched induces excessive body tension, followed by twisting, resulting in painful abrasions to the skin. Get salt into it and you will know about it. Hold both head and tail in the same hand, leaving the other free for disgorging. Hook removed, curse the thing, even threaten it if you must, then put it back.

Correct dogfish handling.

Bull Huss

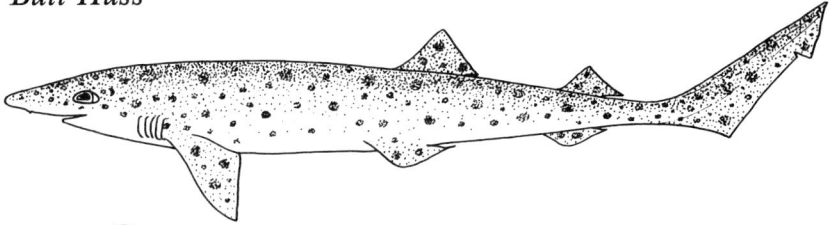

Bull Huss – Scyliorhinus stellaris: rough skinned and well spotted, bull huss are similar to lesser spotted dogfish, differing in that its nasal flaps are large and do not touch the lip. Colouration: variable according to terrain. So too are the markings, though often they take the forms of large spots well spaced over a light brown to pinkish background.

In every sense of the word this is a dogfish, but because of its greater potential for growth, presenting itself as perhaps the biggest fish a great many sea anglers will ever latch onto with ease, bull huss have earned themselves a reasonable degree of respectability. Like their lesser spotted cousins, they show a tendency to gulp down better-intentioned fish baits, chafe nylon hook lengths and inflict painful abrasions to the skin. Huss appear somewhat thinner on the ground than little spotties, seemingly preferring deeper water covering sand, shingle, boulders and even heavy reefy ground. Terrain type in fact has some bearing on actual coloration and markings. Text book huss always appear sandy to pink, with a well-dispersed scattering of big spots interspersed with small flecks, becoming closer and darker on the upper back. More often than not that patterning spells patchy stony ground. I've had quite a few biggies out of Looe while reefing for conger and bream, from where the 21-3-0 record was taken back in 1955. These fish were very finely spotted, becoming almost uniform deep brown on their upper parts. Very big huss are not uncommon over really heavy ground.

Well-scented baits are very important in drawing in huss, especially after dark. Oily fish strips fished on or near the bottom are best. Bigger fish obviously prefer bigger meals. On many marks this is an open invitation to other fish of like habits, but with teeth enough to part nylon. Bull huss themselves make no real trace material demands. Still, in the interest of minimising hook bite-offs by tope, light calibre steel is advisable. Choose hooks to suit the projected general run of fish expected. Huss can get their mouths around anything up to 10/0s. Getting the hook in is no problem. Getting it back out often can be. Pliers and even minor surgery may well be needed, as dogfishes possess exceptionally tough mouths. As far as keeping for the table goes, if rock salmon turns you on, then these are the fish for you.

Monkfish

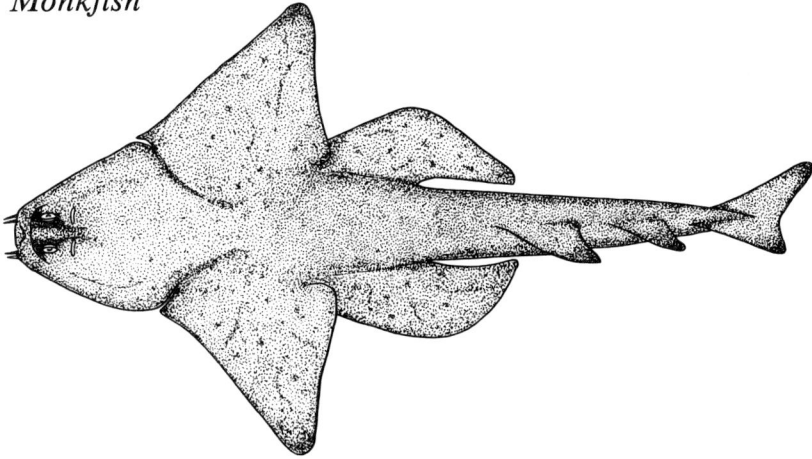

Monkfish – Squatina squatina: a rather obvious fish. A sort of link between sharks and rays with features mid way between the two. Only the anglerfish comes anywhere near in appearance, its large mouth being situated on top as opposed to underneath. Colouration: greyish to sand brown with variable markings.

Constantly unpredictable, it would be wrong to label the monkfish specifically as a charter, dinghy or shore angler's fish. Seemingly, no one faction is able to outdo the rest. Large expanses of clean to mixed ground bring in a few, chomping their way through, rather like large slow animate vacuum cleaners. Personally, I have yet to catch one. Friends who have tell of a slow, rather weary, pumping struggle with no real spirit. Rare indeed are venues offering a regular chance of success. Only Fenit in Eire has this distinction. Back in the UK, fair numbers turn up in Cardigan Bay, South Wales and around the outer Solent. North Cornwall is not without potential either, though little attention is paid to tactics liable to give a result. The interesting thing about monkfish is that they represent the link between sharks and rays. This entire group is distinct from our more regular fishes in having neither fin rays or bones. What shape they have is built upon a framework of cartilage. Some are round, others flat, with monkfish being neither one or the other. As to be expected, its life style is governed by this fact. Always willing to follow a strong scent trail leading up to a slice of mackerel or herring, just as long as it isn't positioned too far from reach of bottom. One point of interest here, is that less reputable fishmongers have in the past been known to turn monkfish tails into what they pass off as scampi. Obviously an excellent table fish, and potentially a very big fish regularly topping 30lbs, the record standing at 66 pounds.

Thornback Ray

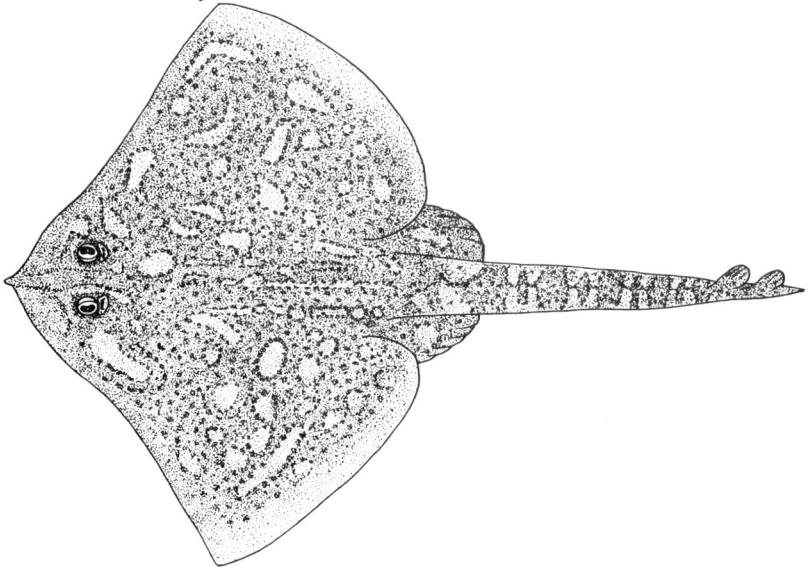

Thornback Ray – Raja clavata: a very variably marked fish with an ability to mimic others, particularly rays with spots. In its natural colouration the upper surface ranges between grey and greeny brown with a mottled, marbled patterning. The main give-away is the variable scattering of large, broad based spines or thorns, hence the origin of the name.

The catching of rays differs little from species to species. Only locational factors bring varieties other than thornbacks into the reckoning. Fish for one, and like it or not, you are fishing for them all. Whether or not a good mix is on the cards is another thing. Thornbacks dominate much of the inshore scene north, south, east and west, from shallow to deeps, over sand and stones. Being flat, they are obviously none too keen on rocks. But, like dabs, an odd one might set up home on a tiny sprinkling of sand bounded by rocks on all sides. I remember lifting one from a black bream mark that had already claimed a number of terminal tackles. Thornbacks are the first of the so-called bigger summer species back inshore towards winter's end after being one of the last to depart around late autumn. A sixteen pounder picked up a mackerel strip of mine off Fleetwood two days before Christmas. Was it an early homecomer or a late leaver? Very likely, early season forerunners will be good ones, often in the high teens, remaining in small shoals at first. Probably close grouping of their foodstuffs plays a big part here. Later, as food spreads itself about, so greater freedom of movement is offered to the fish. Given a free choice, thornbacks favour stony ground intersected by deep gullies cutting across shallow-lying banks, with fish feeding on the tops and upper slopes around top water, and deeper down the gullies towards the bottom of the ebb. Powerful crushing jaws show much of what rays hunt during the normal course of events. Crabs and shellfish are no problem, with opportunist meals of worm or small fishes taking second place. Fish baits on simple nylon or light steel flowing traces are standard practice on ray sorties, but only because anglers consider the better alternatives too demanding in the gathering. If we could ask the fish themselves, they would tell a different story. One of my best thornback catches came after dark on peeler crab. Rays feed particularly well at night. Fish baits however will do a very good job.

The single most important fact to remember with all rays is their tremendous ability to track down baits by scent. Rubby-dubby would be a logical step here. Baits oozing juice down tide draw in the fish, which explains why on charter trips everyone makes a scramble for the back. Twelve baits laying down a mini-chum slick will do much to pull in a few rays, which obviously find the stern baits first. Neat-looking offerings mean little in this particular instance; pulling power is what it's all about. Oily baits cut from a herring or mackerel always do well. Sprats too are effective, at times even more so than the others. The trouble is that as they are soft, they are liable to come adrift easily before getting into action. One way around this is to use them frozen from a cool box, allowing sea water to thaw them when in position. Rays work very close to the bottom, smothering their food until it can be carefully manipulated into the mouth. This is where many people mess the whole thing up, mis-reading those early rod movements, and pulling the hook clear instead of waiting to drive it home. Give a taking fish time. One very successful Fleetwood charter skipper used to advise his clients to have a brew, or smoke a cigarette before picking up the rod. To be sure, it would be impossible to wait too long. Hopefully, a fish will start to move off after flopping about for a bit. Put the reel on ratchet if you like. When a fish does start to make off, thumb the spool tight, sinking the hook home. Normally, most will do the job for you. I've known times when thornbacks have simply been on the end when I began winding in for a bait check. This happened a few times off Ainsdale when Brian and I had 48 thornbacks and over 30 tub gurnards between our two boats. Just how long they had been there hooked and gone to ground is anybody's guess. Areas of fair tidal activity attract them, yet strangely enough, much of their feeding will be confined to an hour or so either side of and including low water.

Thornbacks try to match their basic coloration and patterning to whatever it is they are living over. This can be very variable, with every so often, as if specially to confuse people, one will adopt the markings of another species. Rumours have been circulated as to the authenticity of the current 38lb record as nothing has even approached this weight for years. Press stories often make mention of so-called record fish which never materialize in the list. Blonde, spotted and sandy rays are the most mimicked, even to the point of having just the right balance prickles and spines. It would take a very clever fish to put one over on a cuckoo ray. Thorns apart, all rays have a rather soft spine-free area close to the eyes and

snout, just big enough for a thumb at one side and finger at the other for safe lifting. Tails invariably carry the worst concentrations of big spines. Never attempt to pick up a ray by its tail, even with a rag wrapped round it and avoid the jaws during disgorging. Although the teeth are not sharp, they can still make a nasty mess of unwary fingers.

Blonde Ray

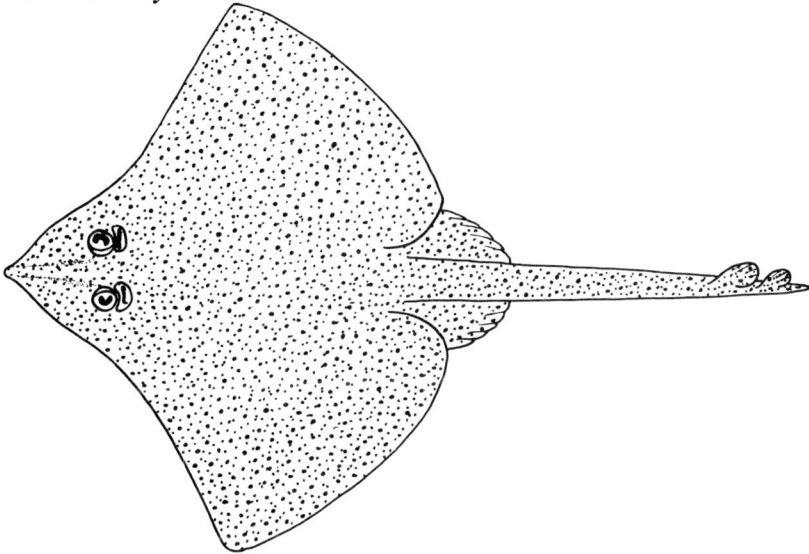

Blonde Ray – Raja brachyura: a fish with short prickles extending over the entire upper surface. In colouration, it is often very much paler than similar fish, being pale sandy fawn, with small uniform black spots extending to the extreme edges of the body.

One of the largest rays in British waters with more 30lb plus specimens caught these days than thornbacks, the current record standing at 37-12-0 off Start Point. Very much a fish of tidal banks surrounded by deep water; turbot territory in fact. Dartmouth boats working the Skerries and Lannacombe area pick up good numbers each summer on turbot/bass tackle as the tide drops away. Some of the banks around Salcombe and Bolt Tail also hold a good head. Newquay is another producer. Further north, boats fishing the Constable Bank spreading out from Amlwch to Conway see a few, and big ones too. Inshore, smaller specimens occasionally get caught. Very much a ray to be deliberately fished for, but off shore.

Dave Lill displays the correct ray handling position of this fine Luce Bay twenty pounder.

Spotted Ray

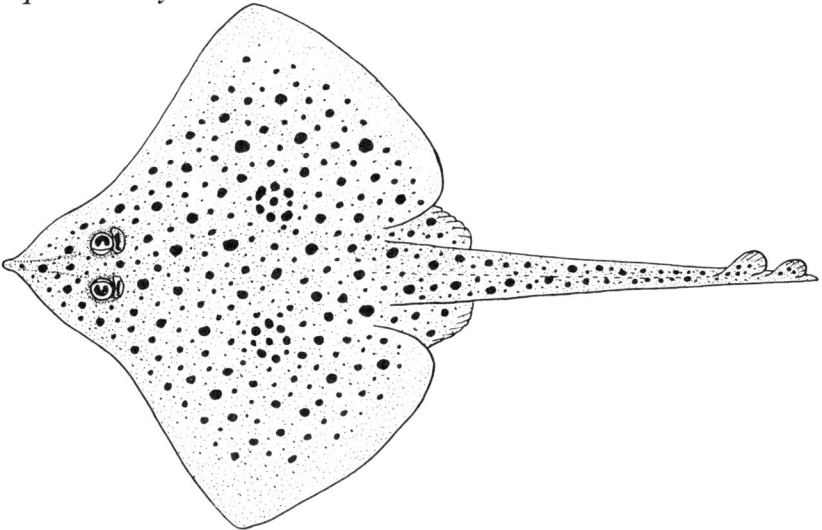

Spotted Ray – Raja montagui: confusion is common between this fish and the similar blonde ray. Both have spots. In this case the spots are of irregular size and do not reach the edge of the wings, creating a plain band. What prickles there are cover only the front part of the upper surface. Colouration: sandy brown with black spots.

Not an abundant fish, but quite widespread, at times quite close to shore. By careful note-keeping over the years, it has been possible to pin point a number of specific venues, these being Loch Ryan, Drummore, Outer Plymouth Sound, Tralee and the western Solent. Some years ago I held the British and Scottish record at 5-2-0 with a fish taken inside Loch Ryan, a fish long since put into the shadows by the current record of 6-14-0. Anglers from the other dinghies insisted it was just a small Blonde, but I wasn't having any of it. Shortly after my fish was give official approval, the press carried a spate of specimen reports and later, a new shore record report, all from the Loch. My fish was caught on a fresh blowlug offered on a two hooked flowing trace also carrying a mackerel strip. Occurrences like this are not uncommon. Though they will take a small fish bait, worm is often shown preference. With my fish on board, I held it finger and thumb in the recognized manner, its tail wedged between my knees. As I reached towards the hook, out shot its lips to meet me halfway. Rays have a tremendous sensory capacity on their under parts. Though it had not seen my hand, it certainly knew it to be there.

Cuckoo Ray

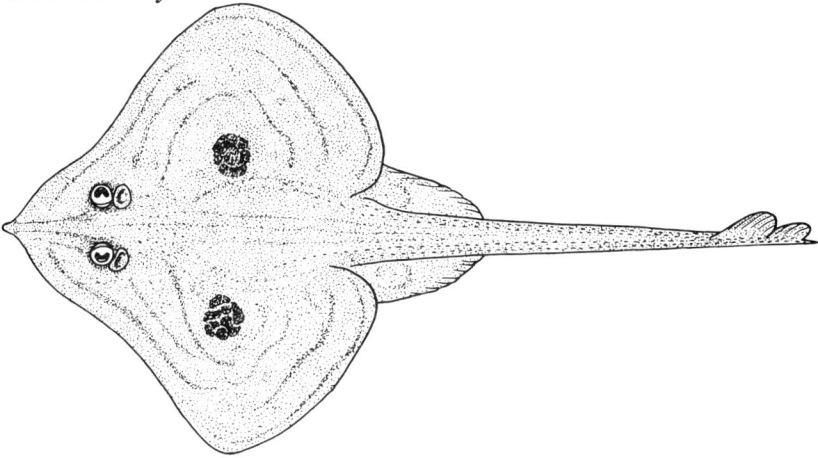

Cuckoo Ray – Raja naevus: perhaps the most readily recognisable ray with its rounded wings and single black and yellow spot (ocellus) on each side. The upper surface is covered with fine prickles. Colouration: sandy yellow.

Another of the smaller rays, well distributed in deep water but never very common anywhere. Only a handful of spots around Britain produce on any sort of regular basis, luckily, most with some dinghy potential. Northern Ireland's Causeway coast, Gourock on the Clyde, Drummore in Luce Bay, and to a lesser extent Cardigan Bay in Wales show fair numbers taken on the rod. A Causeway fish holds the record at 5-11-0. I would say our most outstanding venue of them all is Arran. My friend Neil McLean catches them there, British and Scottish records included, fishing just out of Lamlash on the east side of the island. Without doubt, the easiest ray to hang a name tag on, with its single black ocellus slap in the middle of each wing.

Small Eyed Ray

Where it is found, the small eyed or painted ray is quite a common fish. Simply, it follows a localised, patchy distribution, putting it out of reach of most of us. Southern and Western regions, the Welsh side of the Bristol Channel and down to Lands End see the bulk of the fish. Into the English Channel, some banks off Salcombe, Bolt Tail and Dartmouth attract a good head, the western Solent being more or less the eastern barrier. It would appear that fierce tides are no deterrent. A lot are taken by shore rods fishing surf beaches at low water, or from rocky headlands looking out onto clean patches. Even when the charter boats seek them out in the Bristol Channel, great lumps of lead are required to pin baits down. Dinghy anglers could, if

Identification markings of blonde, spotted and cuckoo rays.

Small Eyed Ray

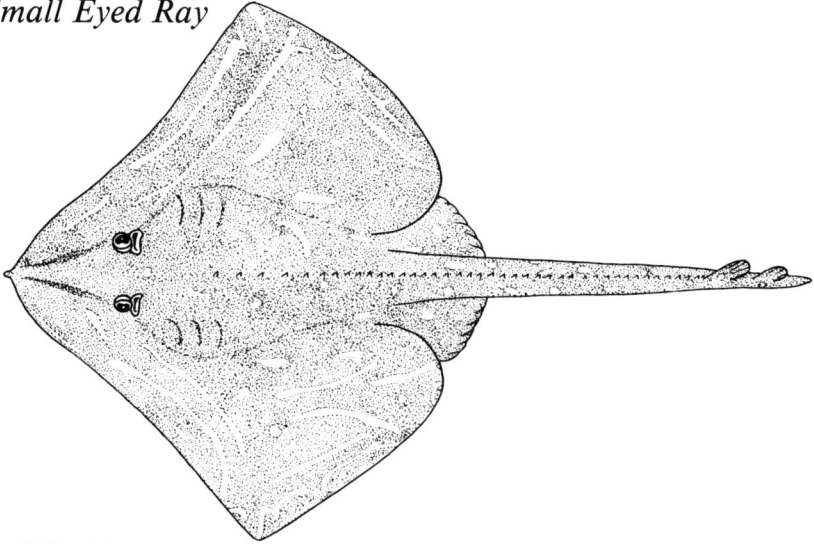

Small Eyed Ray – Raja microocellata: also known as the painted ray. As the name suggests, the eyes are rather small. What prickles there are lie spread about the front half of the body. Colouration is the main feature. Base colours vary between greyish to brown. It is the patterning that counts – white lines and spots in the main running parallel to the outer body shape.

they tried, get amongst more small-eyes than they at present do. For the moment, not a common small boater's target fish. Harry Pout holds the record with a fish of 16-4-0 from the same Salcombe grounds which produced his record blonde ray.

Stingray

A ray by name, but certainly not by nature. Stingrays are summer visitors to muddy, marshy and estuarine areas such as the outer Thames and Solent. Many places receive sporadic, fleeting, even minor regular attention. Our native Lancashire coast turned up an unrivalled spate back in the summers of '77 and '78, yet here is a fish of supposedly widespread potential. Unlike other rays which present little more than token bottom hugging resistance, stingers take off with great authority. I have even seen one become airborne, clearing the surface by a good eighteen inches before powering off back towards bottom; no sulking in the mud for these fellows. At first glance it would be difficult to visualize how such power could be turned on from what on the face of things is a regular looking ray, and a small one at that. On a disc size comparison, stingrays often weigh more than half as much again as regular rays due to power in depth. By this I mean their almost pyramidical height when viewed end on, their high backs blending into powerful shoulders giving great strength to those short stumpy wings. Usually, the

Stingray

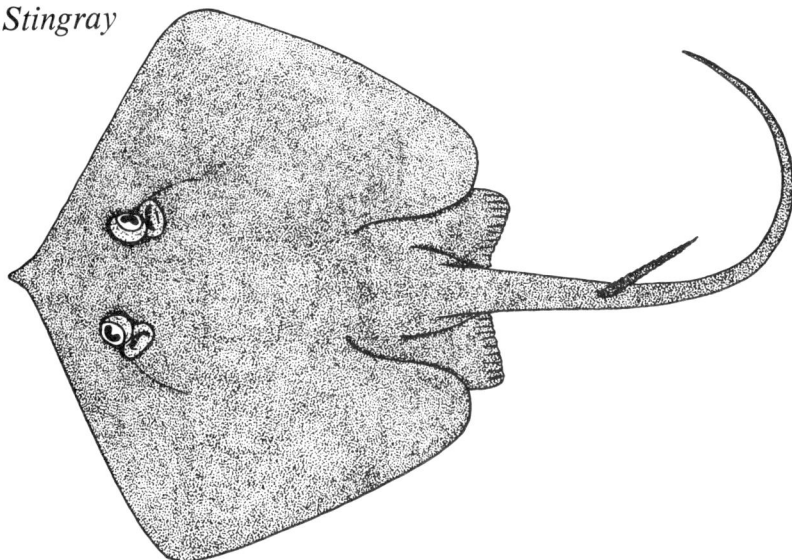

Stingray – Dasyatis pastinaca: unlike the other rays, the stingray has neither back spines nor dorsal fins. A very thickly set fish, often far heavier than its size might suggest. The toothed 'sting' on the tail immediately identifies it. Colouration varies between dark grey and olive brown, without any markings.

forerunners turn up inshore as early as May, peaking some time in June, before dropping into steady decline as the late summer sets in. Britain lies at the northerly extent of stingray range. Much further south around the Canary Islands and north Africa, fish topping 200 pounds are not unknown. The British record stands at a respectable 61-8-0, though obviously there is much potential for improvement. With such a love of warm sub-tropical waters, I can't for the life of me see any reason why they should want to depart our inshore waters as they warm to their seasonal peak, unless it is to do with breeding. I once had a late summer fish lay an egg in the bottom of my boat. I have a friend down in Hampshire who is a stingray specialist. Dink LeMoignan fishes a dinghy out from Beaulieu into the Solent night after night during the summer months, looking for stingrays and smooth-hounds. With fish topping 40 pounds and as many as five in a sitting, Dink obviously knows just what he's about. He favours deep water during the hours of fading light, tucking close inshore after dark. As for tactics, a bunch of ragworms head-nicked onto a bronzed 4/0 fished down tide on a simple nylon flowing trace does all the damage. Takes show as a steady run against the ratchet. As stingrays have no culinary value, on top of giving great sport, there is no reason not to set them free. Anyway, who wants a six inch serrated needle sharp spine on the end of a whip-like tail lashing around them in an enclosed space after dark? Most of Dink's fish are cut free

Spine from a stingray's tail. The forward pointing serrations are likely to do more damage coming out than going in.

outside the boat, hence the bronzed hook which will eventually rust away. When, occasionally, a big one is kept for weighing, it is killed with its head on the gunwhale long before the rest of its body comes aboard, then is sandwiched between a couple of fish boxes just in case. Fortunately, stingers die comparatively easily.

Many fine specimens are caught from small boats working the Thames estuary. Bradwell in particular springs to mind when fishing the river close to the power station warm water outflow. My own catching experiences are limited to western Solent waters, both with Dink's, and later from my own boat appropriately named Stinger. Our best specimens have only been average fish in the twenties, not huge fish, but handful enough. Quite an unmistakeable ray in that its thickly set, slimy, brown green upper surface is, with the obvious exception of the tail, spine free.

Thick Lipped Grey Mullet

Mullet, despite being true sea fish, present their best angling opportunities to shore rods around piers, harbour walls and well into estuaries. A freshwater run-off very often plays a crucial role. In a small boating context, much of what can be achieved afloat will probably be matched or even bettered from dry land. Not that this should necessarily pull the rug out from anyone wishing to give it a go, particularly when gales prevent everything else. Access to spots unfishable on foot can occasionally be had. Otherwise, mullet fishing is mullet fishing however you do it, demanding freshwater float tactics worked through a blanket of groundbait. Christchurch harbour immediately springs to mind. Often when walking early in the morning I would see small punts anchored out in the main basin beyond the lines of moored yachts. The lads were always bait fishing with what at a glance

Thick Lipped Grey Mullet

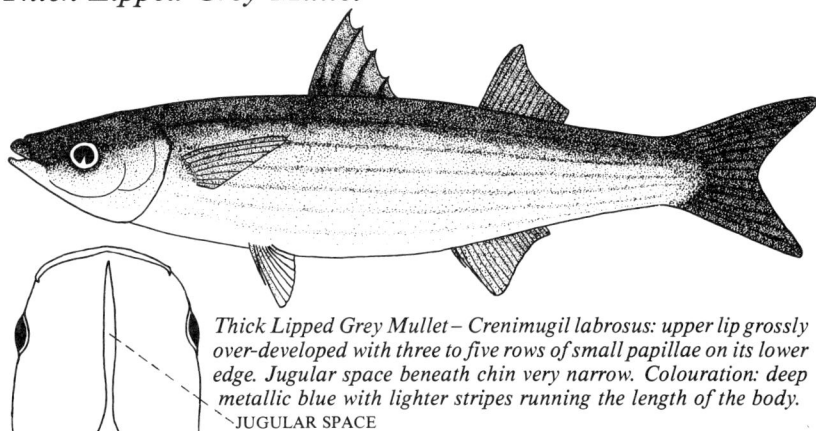

Thick Lipped Grey Mullet – Crenimugil labrosus: upper lip grossly over-developed with three to five rows of small papillae on its lower edge. Jugular space beneath chin very narrow. Colouration: deep metallic blue with lighter stripes running the length of the body.
JUGULAR SPACE

appeared to be match tackle, taking a number of fish averaging 2-3lbs. Occasionally, bigger fish were caught, but none coming anything like close to the 10-1-0 record boated off nearby Portland. Bait choice varied with whatever was being laid down as an appetizer. At times, this is done naturally by the outflow pipes of food processing factories, or trawlers dumping offal. Over in the Isle of Man, the kids use fish heads as combined swim feeders and weights. Tied to the line a little way above, a tiny mackerel bait fixed to a size 4 hook looks like a fish particle just having broken free. In moves a mullet, taking it full of confidence.

Down at Looe, I've watched small shoals turn over fish skeletons close by the harbour wall. One shark boat skipper tossed a rubby dubby bag over one morning while still moored and proceeded to hand-line mullet aboard after inducing a feeding frenzy. Otherwise, it is a case of catfood, bread, small ragworm, cheese and the rest. Some of the modern high protein carp baits have also proved their worth. Just remember to bait both hook and swim alike.

In their natural state, mullet feed on a wide variety of microscopic plant forms, probably taking in tiny molluscs and crustaceans more by chance than design. This explains much of their nosing up and down harbour walls, or browsing beneath boat hulls. All have the ability to combat the osmotic effects of freshwater to varying degrees. So freshwater, and its branch of tactics, are very much at home in this context. Conditioning is what mullet fishing is all about, both for the angler and his fish. There is one other approach deserving of mention before closing, though not necessarily a good idea everywhere. Ever heard of mullet spinning? Not that they go for a flashing blade; ragworm has to be applied to the treble, after which the fishing is as prescribed for any other facet of spinning. Only in specific areas is it successful, though you will never know if you never try. A method to be either lethal, or a complete and utter waste of time; nothing in between.

Thin Lipped Grey Mullet

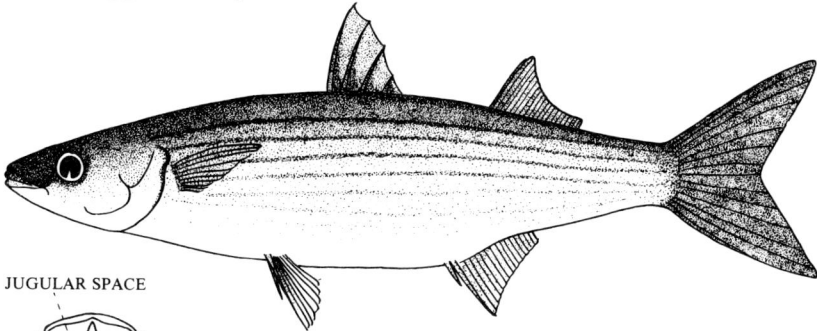

JUGULAR SPACE

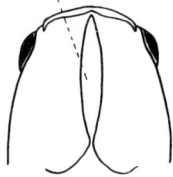

Thin Lipped Grey Millet – Liza ramada: upper lip very narrow, pectoral fin when folded forward does not reach the eye. Mullet are best distinguished by checking the jugular space beneath the chin. In this instance it is wide. So too is that of the rarer golden grey mullet, but its pectoral fin when folded forward passes well beyond the edge of the eye. Colouration: deep metallic blue with lighter stripes running the length of the body.

When I used to watch those chaps mentioned earlier bait fishing for mullet at Christchurch, on an odd occasion, somebody would pick up a couple on baited spinner. As already mentioned, where mullet spinning is effective, it can be extremely successful. With only an odd one being landed, I concluded that the people in question could not be covering sufficient fish. By this time I had already done much stingray and smoothhound fishing in the Solent, and it seemed then a good idea for the following year to trail my own boat. The journey would not be wasted no matter what the weather, with the mullet offering a fallback. This I did in July 1980. Just after dawn, armed with a box of ragworm, 2 gram Jenspin lures, a tub of large split shot and a light spinning rod apiece, Keith Philbin and I nosed our way down the River Stour without any clue of just where we were going. Great patches of reeds fringing shallow muddy bays looked attractive, but obviously only to us, and not the fish. Up, down, here and there, we cast about totally rewardless. The tide was running off fast, eventually stranding us on a shallow flat. Up to our knees in mud, we somehow managed to slide the boat back into the remaining channel. As it was breakfast time, we decided to give it just ten minutes, during which time, eight mullet saw the inside of the boat. Eager for a repeat, next morning we were back, but remained fishless until the tide outside began to flood, holding up the river. A pattern quickly developed. As the water inside hit its lowest level, the fish had nowhere else to go except for the narrow main channel. They were in ravenous mood. By anchoring the boat in the narrowest bottleneck available, we simply picked them off passing through.

Trevor Housby came along with us towards the end of our stay. That day we boated around 35 fish. To be honest, I was so taken up with the general sport and getting fish back quickly, I failed to notice that the bulk were thin lips, not thicks. It was Trevor who mentioned it in passing. He had kept back some of the better ones, first for his camera, then for his wife. Back home, I scouted through the record list and was amazed to read of the boat records being open at two pounds. Most of the fish taken had topped this weight. A phone call to Trevor sent the best in his freezer on its way for identification. Sadly, it didn't arrive. Of course, our talk of dozens of unsubstantiated record fish was greeted with an obvious response. Determined to show everyone, it was back the following year. Every session produced good fish. Young Ian took top honours, along with five of the next best six. Steve Lill, my crew mate who had taken the previous year's best, put enough records into his landlady's freezer to ensure no repeat fiasco. Later, Bruce Vaughan and Tom Quinn from *Sea Angling Monthly* joined us, Tom matching Ian's best on the royal wedding day, and both went on to be equal record holders.

Other fleeting visits have since been made, with Marion Wisdom upping the record a little further. Inevitably, local anglers cottoned on, pushing the record up beyond three pounds. There is scope for a further increase yet, certainly to well above four pounds. When this happens, it will be a fish either from Hampshire, or east Sussex. Sadly, thin lipped mullet are somewhat localised. Mind you, spinning is not the only useful method; far from it. The bulk of all thin lips fall to conventional float tactics and tiny harbour rag. We tried static baits, but could only catch flounders, eels and bass. Our spinners also lured a few nice bass around six pounds, which, on four pound line, provide even more of a handful than mullet.

Conger

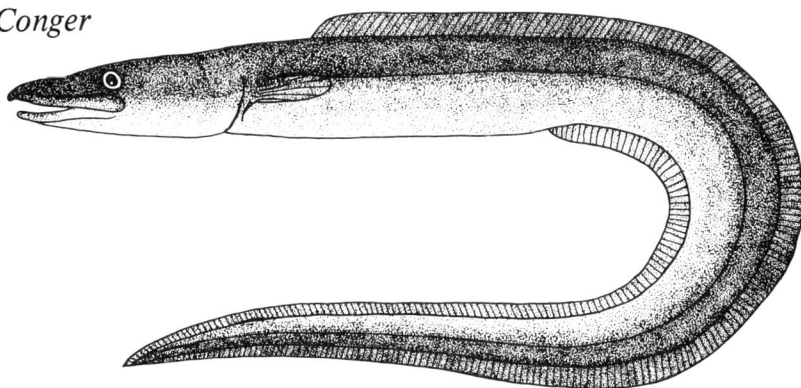

Conger – Conger conger: distinguished from the similar silver eel by the upper jaw being longer than the lower, its pectoral fin being pointed and the origin of the dorsal fin being close to the tip of the pectoral fin. Colouration: varies according to water depth. Usually deep slatey-grey on the upper parts, but can be very pale indeed.

Marion Wisdom and Norman Iddon with a brace of record thin lipped mullet.

A name sure to strike fear into the hearts of the masses, especially those living off hearsay. Old wives tales abound concerning damaged limbs, missing fingers, chewed waders and a host of similar – for the most part exaggerated – nonsensical remarks. Conger do have teeth, although they are small and way out of proportion to any stories concerning them. What conger do possess are strong jaws. That they will bite or take a firm grip goes without saying. Show me a fish that won't have a chew on fingers fool enough to be poked inside its mouth. Conger are, when treated properly, no more mean or aggressive than most other large predators. They are simply another fish capable of giving a good day's sport. Granted, a really big one could be a handful in a small boat, but no more so than tope, and I've had some rare old exploits with 40 to 50 pound tope snapping around my heels. Perhaps thankfully, small boat rods are rarely responsible for really big eels. With fish up to thirty pounds or so, I would not think twice in having them aboard.

A high proportion of inshore conger lean towards the teens of pounds; what a job trying to scoop them up in a landing net! Working from the other end things get worse. I am no gaff fan, but this is one fish, provided I wanted it for eating, which normally I do not, where the case for a gaff could be argued. Not that it would necessarily make much difference. Most 'strap conger' will fit into the 'U' bend, sliding clear. As I say, we do not often keep the things. Light hook holds are easily severed by allowing your eel to spin or shake itself free. Deeply hooked fish get trace-hauled aboard. Most can be held for long enough around the back of their heads until ready for throwing back. Some people rate them for eating, but they certainly take some killing. My advice in this case is drop them straight into an open sack or plastic bag, tying the top. Cut the trace and start again. you can retrieve your tackle later. Sacks not only keep writhing eels at bay, they also make for a slime-free deck and sure footing for the next bundle of fun to come aboard.

Conger behaviour varies greatly from spot to spot. Around Lancashire, small ones pick our tope baits over stones all summer long. Nobody ever seriously bothers with them. Come the backend when the whiting arrive, demanding fish strips, conger start appearing all over the place, possibly due to an increase in hooks carrying mackerel bait. All the eels in the area apparently head closer to shore late in the season, as if in a last ditch effort to get some rich feeding before cooler conditions see them off for another year. Dropping temperatures certainly make for keener appetites, a fact echoed in other parts of the country. Otherwise, tactics are standard. Good, fresh, oily fish baits or small calamari squids presented on yard-long flowing traces will catch 'em all. Use steel if it promotes confidence. Small 'strap eels' can be beaten with heavy monofilament, if you keep an eye out for chafing. In really deep water, conger feed at any stage of the day. Inshore, close, calm, sultry evenings fish best. Nocturnal feeding plays an important part in a conger's life cycle, bringing into play their acute sense of smell. The question of rubby dubby raises itself again. Oily fishbaits catch most, but is it because they are more universally used? Under natural conditions, small pouting rate high on the conger hit list. Fished whole, conger love them. So, this is a sporting and very available fish, not a demon.

Silver Eel

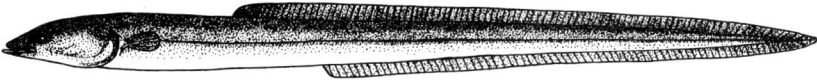

Common Eel – Anguilla anguilla: often found both adjusting to or taking up permanent residence in salt water close to shore, it differs from the conger in having a bottom lip that protrudes longer than the upper. Also, its dorsal fin starts well behind the rather small rounded pectoral fins. Colouration: variable between blackish grey to brown becoming lighter ventrally.

Contrary to popular belief, silver or common eels as they are also known, are not freshwater fish. Neither are they necessarily migrants maturing in freshwater. Granted, most on reaching our coastline after being spawned in the distant Sargasso Sea do enter one of our river systems, then perhaps on to a lake, pond or canal, until the Sargasso beckons them back via our coastal waters to spawn and eventually die. Some, however, decide that coastal waters are just what they always wanted, opting for a permanent life at sea. As the feeding is richer, growth is better, all of which can lead to great confusion. Sea anglers expect to catch a few silver eels from time to time. Near freshwater outlets, they can reach plague proportions, grabbing at more or less anything from shrimps, shellfish or worms, to fish strips and crab put there for better purposes. What a mess they make of both terminal tackle and hands. In the main, these fish are small, probably averaging a pound, a three pounder being a good one. Anything bigger invariably gets labelled small conger. Currently, the freshwater silver eel record stands at 11 pounds 2 ounces. What would it have been labelled had it been taken at sea after a well-fed coastal life? Just how many records have been let slip especially when the record stood at under nine pounds is anybody's guess. A general awareness of this situation could pay dividends in the future. Their catching is simple. Hooks in the region of sizes 1 to 1/0 on the bottom around darkness are the recipe. Be sure and pin the right name to your fish. Unlike conger, silver eels have a protruding lower lip, and small round pectoral fins, well in front of the dorsal and anal fins.

Bass

As a subject, bass fishing is so complex, that we in a book such as this could never hope to do it any sort of justice. Tactically speaking, bassing spans the entire angling spectrum. For example, commercial boats fishing the Christchurch ledge use what can be loosely termed angling methods,

Bass

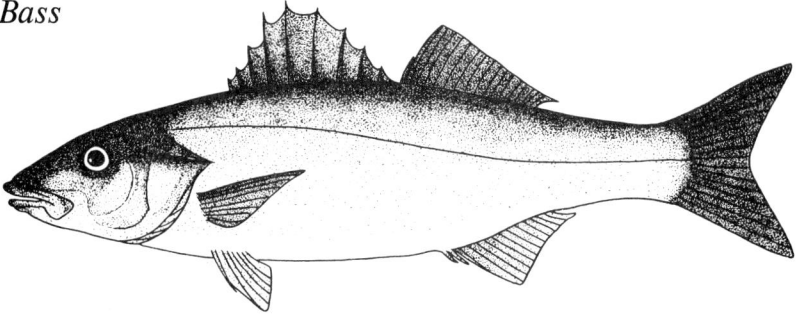

Bass – Dicentrarchus labrax: a very spiney, scaley, powerful metallic looking fish. Its dorsal fins are completely separate and the pre-operculum (situated on the gill cover) has a number of large forward pointing teeth. Colouration: deep greyish blue on the upper parts, becoming silvery and finally white underneath. A black spot on the gill cover may merge into the general colouration.

pumping in handfuls of sand-eels followed by live baits either trotted or deeply float fished to the frenzied fish. Other commercial men troll redgills over shallow reefs such as Eddystone, producer of the 18-6-0 record. Bass can group up naturally anywhere between the bottom and top. Surface shoalers sometimes get betrayed by wheeling gulls picking at the remnants of each frenzied attack on the small fish they drive up. Quietly drifting through a shoal with spinning gear will take a toll of these fish. Conversely, others swarm over offshore banks or harbour sandbars hunting sandeels. Estuaries equally attract their share, many of which fall to spinners and bait, particularly legered crab. Rock fishermen, beach fishermen, boat fishermen, harbour fishermen, even coarse fishermen up on the Royalty section of the Hampshire Avon have all been known to take coveted double figure bass. In recognising that we cannot therefore hope to cover but a fraction of bassing approaches, I propose simply to run through some of my own experiences in the hope that you might relate to them.

Up here in the north west, bass are rarely given a second thought. Probably few people even know they exist. This they most certainly do, and in good numbers, requiring specialist treatment to get any sort of success. Let me say that very shallow offshore banks hold the key and in some cases these dry completely at dead low water on big spring tides. In the interest of safety, never try and work through a maze of gullies on a dropping tide. So shallow can the water get in places, that the passage back could well get cut off, which, on a dodgy forecast might result in all sorts of problems. We weave through at low tide, getting in as close as possible, at times all but running aground. Still some way off, the tide is scouring the sand as it rushes back, evicting all manner of food stuffs. Baits cast along this scour line are what it is all about. I prefer soft crab on a flowing trace to 4/0, leaving the rod propped low against the transom. No messing about with these fish. One second nothing, the next a rod doing its best to climb over the woodwork. In

A lesser weever. Note the erect poison carrying spines of the black first dorsal fin.

this instance, only the first two hours flood provide consistent sport, probably due to the scouring action being lost as the bank covers more deeply, causing fish to meander off in search of larders new.

Drift fishing between Hengistbury Head and Mudeford Quay offers fair small boat bassing, I should say about a mile or so off, moving with the tide, trailing fresh sandeels bought from the returning charter boats at nearby Poole. Beware of plunging unwary hands into the bait tub. I once had a live weever mixed in amongst my sandeels. Always a problem is knowing at just what level to expect fish. I'll admit I was more surprised when I was given two small drilled bullets, which proved to be perfect on the day. It was a breezy, lumpy sort of morning taking the little boat along at a fair rate of knots. Later, as rigor-mortis set into our remaining baits, we decided to try an hour trolling against the tide, which again worked for me. Eventually, the engine, an old inboard petrol model, gave up the ghost. Conditions were deteriorating rapidly. In fact, as everyone else, charters included, ran for home, we looked like being stranded alone. The engine was in bits all over the floor. Finally, a fast cruiser came to our aid, for which he was rewarded with my bass. Take note, though, he could have demanded more; read the section on salvage rights.

Lannacombe Bay close to Start Point holds a good head of bass, again sandeel feeders, working up and down the maze of gullies cut into a large bank surrounded by deep water. With both bottom gradients and water depths varying constantly, plenty of line out is a necessity to maintain bottom contact. Traces too need to be long, up to twenty feet in fact, giving the baits natural movement. Long traces are equally essential when lure trolling. Do not confuse this with lure spinning where the idea is to cast towards the fish. Always, the choice of weighting for any drift is a problem, particularly if feeding levels have first to be ascertained. When unsure, hedge your bets by getting as many different combinations over as possible. As a pattern for the day emerges, everyone swops accordingly, but remember, patterns may change day by day. Of course, it does help to have some idea of the range to be experimenting within. Only local knowledge can dicatate this. A case of either trial and error, or inside information; eat humble pie if necessary and ask.

My final experience takes us back to mullet fishing inside Christchurch harbour. This we did with baited spinners like Mepps or ABU Droppens, cast with light freshwater gear. At the same time, someone would usually have a static bait lobbed out more from curiosity than expectation. Both approaches caught, amongst many other things, bass. Always, though, our better fish fell to spinner. In fact, I'll wager we didn't see bass bettering three-quarters of a pound come to either our own baits, or those cast by others from the nearby shore. Yet we caught bass that topped five pounds. Now I don't do that much deliberate harbour bassing, but I do keep my eyes and ears well open. Seemingly, some tremendous fish creep into harbours towards dark, at times getting caught on small live pouting. Christchurch harbour is actually a reed-fringed basin some way up to the river Stour, full of small freshwater fry. More conventional harbours prove equally attractive to tiny fish, usually gobies, tiny pollack and pout. Perhaps this is what big bass come in looking for; who knows? Certainly from my own experience, static 'dead' baits are, to say the least, not very well received at all. Bass are notoriously slow both in their growing and maturing. At times, it can be difficult to know just what sort of conservational action to take. I have some sympathy with a view expressed by many that fish returned are only going to fatten the wallets of netsmen. Some anglers keep only the bigger fish, preferring to release immature fish of under around 4-5 pounds. My own view is that if a fish is already mature, it must have a better chance of seeding future generations than one with possibly years yet to wait and the risk of being caught. In no way is this intended as a plea to kill small fish in preference to big ones. Just another angle to consider before putting the case for returning all bass, or at most keeping just an odd one per trip, regardless of the others being big. Fortunately, bass fishing has won itself a cult following, the supporters of which see conservation as the single big issue facing them. Good luck to them, and to a species just as much in danger of being helped to the wall now by thoughtless angling action as by any other dangers threatening it: think before you kill.

Black Bream

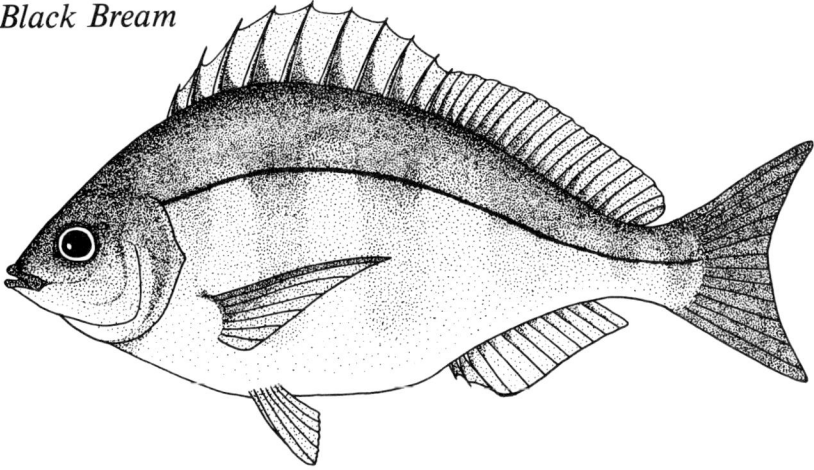

Black Bream – Spondyliosoma cantharus: a laterally flattened, deep bodied fish of metallic appearance. Obviously a sea bream, distinguished from its near relatives immediately by its colouration which leans towards blackish grey with an underlying hint of metallic silver. Darker on the upper parts becoming lighter on the sides, with a series of several dusky vertical bars.

A number of bream species undertake a shoreward migration during the summer months to feed over rocky or broken ground, black bream being no exception. What makes these special in a dinghy sense is the extent to which their inshore run can extend. The call for heavy ground may not be so pronounced either. Patches of broken, weedy chalk are home to many mid-Channel bream, often within reasonable striking range. On the minus side, prolific marks are now a little thin on the ground. Small boat fishing has within its boundaries a great deal of scope. Some dinghies are so seaworthy and well equipped as to put middle range marks well within their grasp, given a decent forecast. This broadens the horizons for other species, as well as bream. The reef off Aberdovy could be fished by small fast boats. I've had some nice bream out there, even close in. They are also common off the Dorset, Hampshire and Sussex coast. Out towards the Needles, bream are always a fair bet. Some of my best bream have been taken in a most unusual manner very close by, just into the Solent. They may well be finicky feeders at times with their small mouths, but I've had them pick up a bunch of ragworm on a 4/0 hook fished on clean ground for stingray. Some evenings the rod tip is never still as they tug, tweak and generally wear a big bait down. Come darkness,fortunately they fade away. No doubt, had we wanted, by fishing specifically for them, some great sport could have been enjoyed. Our minds, though, were on bigger things as black bream, even in specimen doses, rarely exceed five pounds, the record standing at 6-14-4. Fish for them on tackle light enough to ensure they put up one of their famed scraps. For their size, they are dogged, never-say-die fighters, shaking and diving repeatedly as they circle the main line, not unlike big mackerel. Left to their own devices, bream use those powerful jaws and teeth to remove encrusting molluscs from their rocky hold fasts. Baits need not follow this particular trend, but do need to be small, offered on hooks of around size 1. Bigger baits result in plenty of attention but few fish. Those that do eventually end up on the hook come as a result of laborious gnawing of the bait until it becomes a manageable lump. Going small right from the onset means many more fish, if only by limiting the time factor between takes. Tackles presenting baits above the weight work best. Whether it is more sporting to catch fish singly or in a cluster is a matter for personal choice. Two or even three hooks spaced up the line will all be in with a chance, as bream will feed within a yard or so of bottom. It should be said that longer traces allowing thin mackerel or squid natural movement work better. In turn, this calls for a single hook approach to cut out inter-snood tangles. Try a yard of monofilament tied to a french boom. Short snooded multi-hook rigs styled on home-tied mackerel feathers are the tools for fishmongery. Black bream are by nature gregarious fish, a point worth bearing in mind and perhaps exploiting with a small rubby dubby bag.

Tub Gurnard

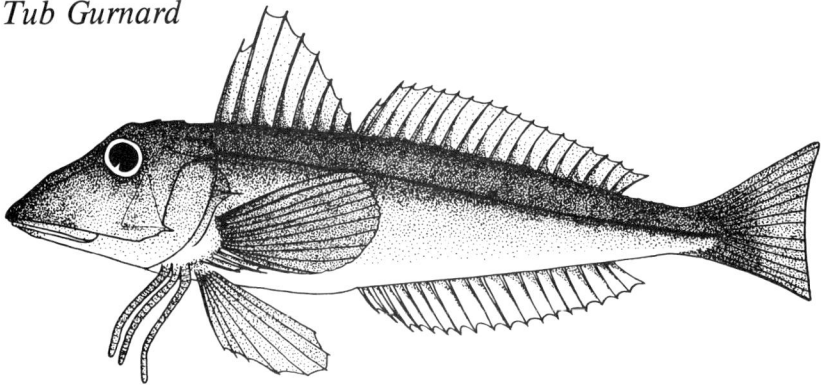

Tub Gurnard – Trigla lucerna: at a glance, often mis-identified as a red gurnard. Basic colouration is indeed red, though very much darker and duller. Both pectoral fins are edged in very prominent bright blue. Check also the lateral line which should be smooth.

Both Brian and I have something of a soft spot for gurnard. Rare indeed are anglers not seeing them as a bonus. Not that we or anyone else for that matter ever set out deliberately to fish solely for them. What we can do is increase the likelihood of an encounter by a few minor tactical alterations to the normal terminal gear. With their odd looking free pectoral rays, gurnard 'walk' along soft sea beds feeling for concealed items of food, which may be a shrimp or a small fish. No sooner are they flushed out than pursued at speed and eaten. Gurnard then are active predators, common in deepish water from around thirty feet or so downwards on clean to patchy ground throughout the summer and autumn months. Three of the four rod recorded species are coloured red, leading to much confusion. How often do we read of 'record' red gurnards? On the official identification table later there unfolds many an untold story. Few ever actually end up on record lists, most being just above average tubs. Here I talk from personal experience. Dinghy fishing in Loch Ryan back in the early seventies I picked up a nice 'red' on mackerel strip. Everyone insisted it was a record red, but without wishing to appear know-it-all, I was not so sure, having read that only tubs had blue-edged pectorals, which this fish had. Anyway, I went along with things. Some weeks later a letter dropped on the door mat confirming my worst fears. My fish was indeed a tub gurnard, and the new official Scottish record at 4-0-8. It does pay then to be fully aware of the situation, record weights included. Had I been absolutely sure, I would have come out of the affair with empty hands.

Not only are tubs the biggest growing, but also the most common gurnard. While others are reputedly common enough, in angling terms their distribution inshore is often patchy. Tubs range the length and breadth of the country. Gurnard fishing is much the same across the species range, as well as being similar to that which is used to catch huss, rays, dogs and the other species commonly sought over similar types of ground. Where tactically it differs is in hook and bait sizes; only an outsized double figure tub like the long standing 11-7-4 record could hope to make any real headway with a tope bait, though perhaps good numbers of 2, 3 and four pound fish might be just waiting to get caught. What you do is tie a mackerel baited 2/0 hook and its short snood to the main 'biggie' trace. Believe me, it can be well worth the trouble. Forget fears of increasing trouble from the problem element. Dogfish are just as capable of gulping down big baits too if they want to. However, if still unconvinced, bait a string of mackerel feathers after the bait bash is complete. Finally, a word or two or warning. Beware those sharp spines and head area which is skinless bare bone, and always use a landing net. Gurnards do not always hook very well. In fact, my record, on taking its first gasp of fresh air in the net, spat out the hook which had only been gripped between its teeth. A beautiful, if rather odd-looking fish, well worth the effort required to put it into the deep freezer.

Red Gurnard

True red gurnards are very much paler and redder than tubs, which is all very well if comparisons can be made. Otherwise, a check of the lateral line will dispel any doubts. Being much smaller – a pound fish is about average, and a three pounder huge, the record standing at 5 pounds – deliberate fishing should be scaled down accordingly. Reds, though they may show anywhere, do prefer slightly deeper water still, with pockets existing along the Atlantic-facing West Country coast, around into the Channel, and fading progressively eastwards. In all other respects, catching reds is as for catching tubs, but with hook sizes down to, at most, size 2/0.

Red Gurnard

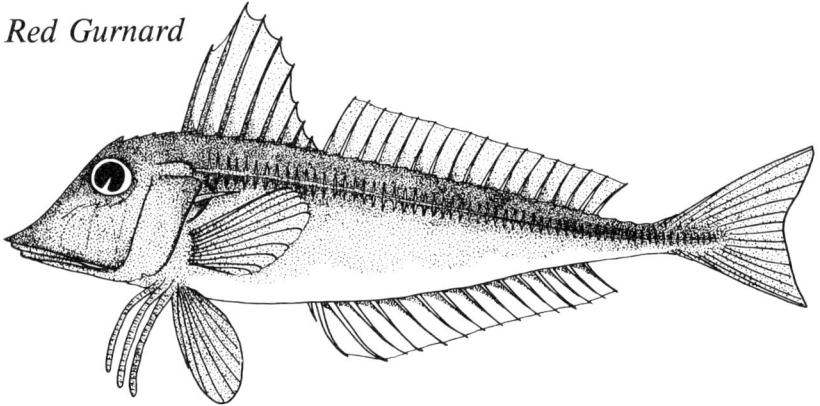

Red Gurnard – Aspitrigla cuculus: blunt head, wedge shaped body and three 'free' pectoral rays distinguish gurnard from all other fishes. The red gurnard differs from the rest in that its pectoral fins just reach the vent. Its lateral line is not toothed, but has soft lateral extensions. Colouration: red (no blue edge to the pectoral fins).

Grey Gurnard

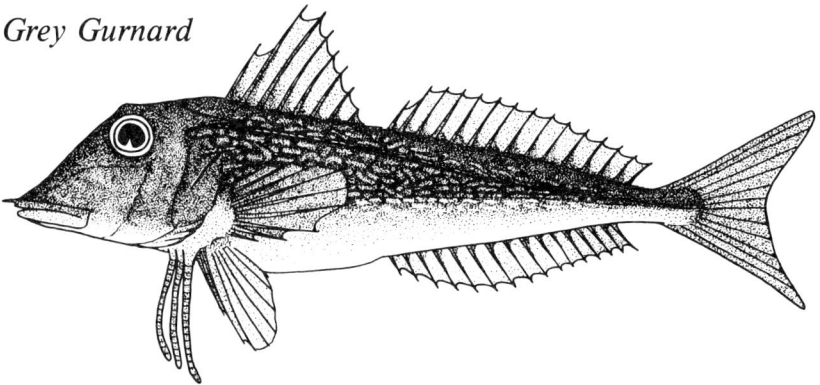

Grey Gurnard – Eutrigla gurnardus: obviously grey, though not always so. Individuals can become pinkish, even red according to diet. Lateral lines determine gurnard identification. In this case, one of sharply pointed scutes. The pectoral fin is short, barely reaching the vent. Often a dark blotch shows on the first dorsal fin.

Our smallest gurnard, often weighing little more than half a pound. Big greys do occur occasionally, mainly in western Scottish waters, from where the 2-7-0 record was taken. Again, fished for like the others, and again with hook sizes scaled down even further to, at most, size 1/0. Worm baits, as well as fish, are taken. I recall a day out in Luce Bay when, after filling the bait box for tope, we put small mackerel strips onto the feathers, bottom bouncing them more in hope of whiting than anything else. At the end of the day, more than forty grey gurnard had been taken. On another occasion I boated one bright red in colour. Baffled at first, I could see it was neither red nor tub. Eventually, after death, its colour faded back to grey. Apparently this is not uncommon, depending on their diet at the time.

Mackerel

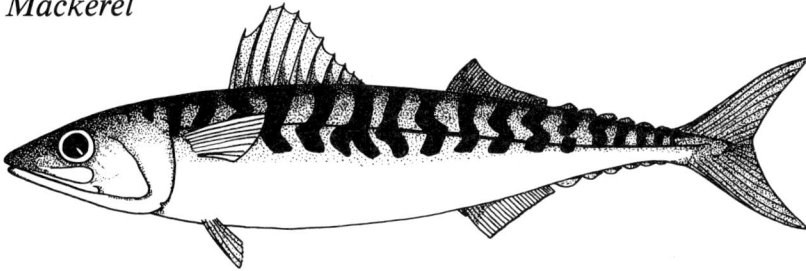

Mackerel – Scomber scombrus: not an easy fish to mistake for any other. A fish of beautiful colouration when alive. The upper back is greeny blue giving way to a white under section. Black curvy bars stretch from head to tail. Then as the light hits it, purple, lilac and other metallic sheens glint from the flanks.

I shouldn't think anyone needs telling that a string of feathers worked sink and draw progressively through the differing water levels right down to the bottom will, given that mackerel are about, satisfy the bait needs of the day. Well, that's the way things used to be in the days before zealous over-cropping and pathetic fisheries policy protection signalled the beginning of the mackerel's end. Nowadays, if you find them, their average size has plummeted. So small, in fact, are the individuals making up some shoals, at Dartmouth recently we kept several alive in an aerated tub to use as bass live baits when the sandeels had all gone. What chance then has the 5-6-8 record now of being broken or average sizes once again topping a pound? On the bait scene, alternatives can be bought. Where angling suffers most is in the resultant loss of other larger predatory fishes no longer being drawn inshore by the disappearing visiting mackerel shoals. Always, enough to ensure they do not go into total extinction will escape the nets. When mackerel decline so far as to become viably uneconomical, large scale netting will have to try wiping out something else instead, but before undertaking any sort of crusade, anglers must be seen not to be hypocritical. There is something about dropping into a shoal of fish in suicidal mood certain to bring out the worst in most of us. A sort of kill-crazy craving takes hold, at the end of which the culprits are often unable even to give away their excesses, let alone eat, use or sell them. As self-appointed champions of preserving angling for the future, we cannot condemn others until our own house is in order. But there is more to mackerel fishing than simply satisfying a demand for bait, it is just a pity really that they are so obliging. Were they to represent a real challenge in the catching specialists would flock down to the coast in search of the fantastic sport mackerel would, and already do, offer. Try landing one on freshwater match tackle with a tiny redgill lure; you will need plenty of line on your reel if the drag is set properly. If not, then wave the fish goodbye. Exploiting their potential is straightforward enough. Simply look for areas of tidal disruption to pin-point the fish, repeatedly drifting over them with small lures. Headlands,

reefs, even piers disturb a steady tidal flow sufficiently well to gather fish. Mackerel always run closest to shore during periods of prolonged summer calm.

Wheeling gulls may betray the presence of a surface feeding shoal. During heavier weather, thick shoals either move off or go into deeper water, keeping clear of the turbulence affecting life close to the top. Should conditions get really bad, shoals can break up completely, scattering far and wide. This presents an interesting slant on the sport fishing aspect, in that the biggest mackerel take on a role of solitary sea-bed hunting. Static baits may well tempt an odd one, but moving baits and lures invariably prove too much to resist. I have seen some cracking specimens up to four pounds fall to drift-fished baits put out for other fish. A similar situation may arise towards the onset of winter. Either dropping temperatures, or the first of the backend gales, will push more run-of-the-mill fish into fleeing towards their traditional wintering grounds. Big fish always do things at a much more dignified rate, meandering off slowly in the wake of the headstrong, picking up whatever last-minute meals present themselves on the journey. For the most part, this will be beyond the scope even of charter boats, let alone dinghies. However, in a few deep Scottish sea lochs, big fish linger on very late, picking up both baits and lures intended for cod as late as December.

Scad

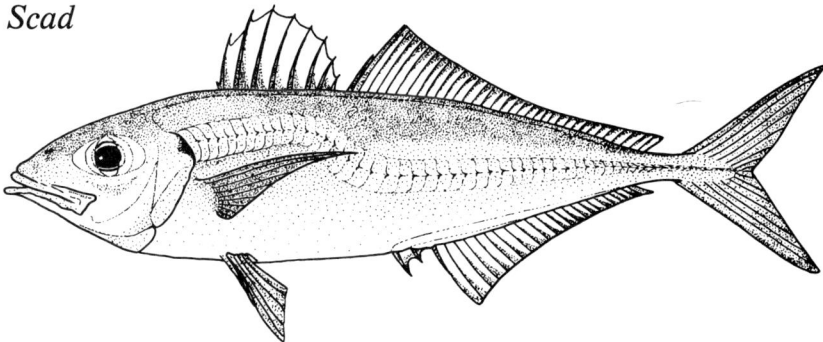

Scad – Trachurus trachurus: a strikingly odd fish on account of its lateral line being crossed by large lateral scutes. Colouration: greenish grey with silvery sides and hints of green. Underparts white. A small black spot appears on the upper gill cover.

Also known as horse mackerel, scad form huge shoals during the warmer months. Settled weather can bring them right up to the shoreline where they hunt small fishes around headlands or up to harbour walls, seemingly attracted by bright lights at the end of the stonework at night. Few boat anglers ever deliberately fish for scad. None-the-less, a lot end up on the deck having taken a fancy to string of feathers or small fish and worm baits. At times, vast shoals invade the inshore marks averaging a pound or so apiece, far outweighing any limited value the odd one might have as either

Gone are the days when mackerel of this size were reasonably expected to take every lure on a trace.

bait or a day saver when the going gets tough. The fact is, scad are another of those fish to be endured out afloat, in particular in the west country. If you are lucky, they might give you a miss.

Garfish

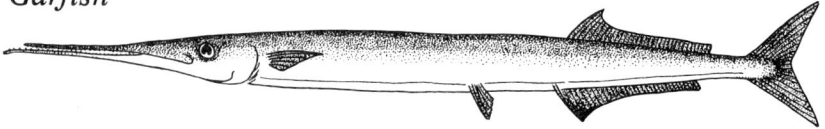

Garfish – Belone belone: elongated shape and beaked jaw is sufficient for immediate identification. The skipper, a rarer but similar fish, has small finlets between its tail and dorsal and anal fins. Garfish colouration: greenish blue becoming silver on the flanks and underparts.

Garfish playing and jumping over the anchor rope are a sure sign that summer is with us again. They fall readily to every item in the mackerel catcher's armoury. In fact, most rod caught gars rate as accidental catches on mackerel feathers. From the shore they are quite common where rocks and piers allow casting into deep water, which means small boats have the perfect opportunity to get the very best from these fun fish. Sadly, few people seem interested in them. Either that or they are totally unaware that garfish hunt in the upper layers, well away from normal baits. Trying specifically for garfish would detract little from the normal course of bottom fishing. On the hook, spectacular sport is assured even with fish averaging around a pound, especially when tackle is light. Out of the water they come like mini-aerobatic swordfish in a bid to be rid of the hook. With the bottom rods set in position, spinning or float trotting tiny mackerel strip just beneath the surface would not interfere. To get inside that beaked, rather small mouth, hooks of no more than size 2 are called for. Personally, I use hooks size 4.

As highly efficient near surface predators, garfish are readily attracted to things that either flash, or provide a strong scent. Spinners satisfy the first demand, and what I have in mind for the second is deliberate ground-baiting. Sharking boats with their surface level rubby dubby bags attract great shoals of gars down tide. So prolific can they be that in the Scillies we had them taking right next to the hull, grabbing tiny belly cuts of mackerel on the drop before our floats even had time to settle. A small onion bag full of crushed mackerel heads and guts shaken regularly over the stern would bring gars flocking to the baits. Some say garfish even make good eating, although I can't comment, never having tried one. In the main, I catch them when I'm on holiday somewhere, without cooking facilities. If you don't mind green bones, give one a try, otherwise mind how you hold them as their scales dislodge very easily. Be sure and carry a good disgorger capable of working in very tight corners. I'll wager that after a taste of the antics light tackle gars put up, those bottom rods will not get a second thought.

Ballan Wrasse

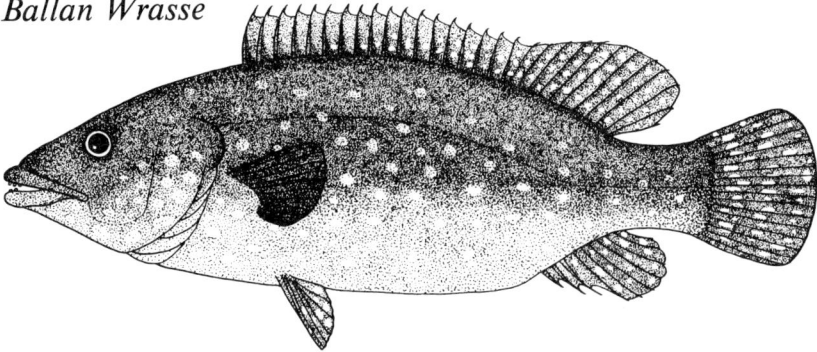

Ballan Wrasse – Labrus bergylta: a well proportioned powerful-looking fish. Two basic colourations exist, depending on locality. Northern fish lean towards green and brown mottling, while southern fish can be any colour from dull shades to bright orange covered in large white or yellowish spots. Britain has two other similar wrasses. Ballans lack the tail stalk black spot of the corkwing, and the fine strong anal spines of the rock cook. As both these other fish are exceptionally small species, confusion with small ballans shouldn't matter anyway.

There is an unwritten rule in small boat fishing that says if you cannot eat it, why bother trying to catch it? I personally do not subscribe to this, but a lot of anglers do. Ballan wrasse are very much victims of this philosophy. Coupled to the fact that they carry a shore angling tag, little, if any, attention is ever paid to them, which is a great pity, as in my considered opinion the small boat approach could put our current specimen and 9-6-0 record under something of a shadow. This said, dinghy wrasse fishing is not for the beginner. Wrasse are lovers of the wildest, rockiest, kelpiest , most inhospitable ground imaginable, much of which lies so close to shore as to be hazardous in some instances. Headlands and cliffs often tower up from the swelly waters. Shore anglers, though they catch good fish, face two disadvantages readily overcome from a boat. Firstly, because wrasse prefer deepish water, baits cannot be made to settle just where they are wanted. Casting over the right bit of submerged jungle is one thing, combating the angle of drop into deep water is quite something else. Problem number two comes after somehow managing to place your bait in a potentially productive spot. As soon as a good fish is hooked, away it powers in search of the nearest, and usually snaggiest, bit of cover around. Even if you can coax it out, the ensuing struggle is fraught with all manner of tackle-hungry obstacles, some of which could easily chafe the line. From a small boat, these problems are cut at a stroke.

I have spent a lot of time wrasse fishing around Peninnis Head in the Scilly Isles. Within yards of the rocks, the water is so deep as to ensure even the best cast line ends up back down at your feet. Consequently, all my fish were feeders from along the rock face. Odd ones went as big as four pounds, but none of those huge, possibly double figure, fellows thought to lurk in

Scilly waters. Eventually I got a boat to take me round and anchor up in a small sheltered cove a couple of hundred yards off. Here the water depth was tremendous, covering the most snaggy ground I have ever fished in all my life. But we got good fish. Conditions dictated that tackle rigs be kept simple. A single snood some three feet above the weight proved adequate. The greater the number of tackle bits hanging from the trace, the greater the risk of losing it. Even weights could be a problem. Take along anything heavy, such as old nuts, chain links, spark plugs or whatever, any of which could be tied to the trace with a weak sacrifice link in order that tackle losses are minimised. Hook sizes in the region of size 1 are perfect. Baits depend to a large degree on what is available. Oddly enough, the supposedly best wrasse bait, which is a ten-pence-sized hard back crab, was almost non-existent under the rocks. Lugworm did, however, serve as a good substitute. Otherwise, ragworms, limpets, soft-backed crabs and live prawns will all be taken readily. As our experimenting was taken elsewhere in search of other fish on mackerel strip, wrasse seemed equally happy at times to give these a go too.

Cuckoo Wrasse

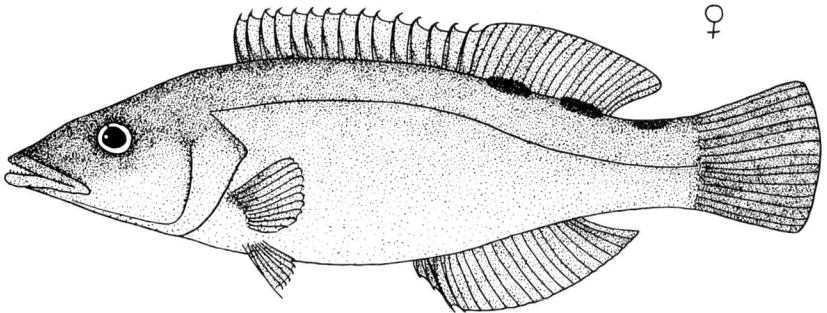

Cuckoo Wrasse – Labrus mixtus: by virtue of some very prominent and beautiful markings, particularly amongst males, a difficult fish to mis-identify. However, due to the great colour variation between sexes, the two have often been put down as separate species. Males have blue heads and backs with yellowy-orange bodies. Their dorsal and anal fins are also yellowy-orange. Females and immature males are plain orange, with three black spots on the back close to the tail. As this fish is an hermaphrodite, fish of intermediate colouration can exist.

Unlike ballan wrasse, cuckoos are a true deep water fish. I have seen an occasional one picked up from the shore, but the moment you get afloat, it's a different matter. Still lovers of really heavy ground, cuckoo wrasse show a decided preference for small strips of mackerel. They average perhaps little more than a pound, the record standing at 2-0-8. Hooks need to be kept small, no bigger than size 2. Otherwise, baits fished above the weight will do fine. With their fantastic markings, they must rate as Britain's most spectacular fish, the males at least, with their blue heads and stripes running over yellow pinkish bodies. Females and immature males bear absolutely no resemblance at all to the males, so much so that it is difficult to believe all belong to the same species. The females are plain pink fish with three dark blotches on the upper back close to the tail. In common with other wrasse, cuckoos serve little purpose other than sport. Take care then not only in handling, but bringing them up as well, for wrasse are highly susceptible to compression problems. With eyeballs bulging and swim bladders blown out through their mouths, throwing them back only condemns them as gull fodder. Bring them up slowly to avoid the bends.

———————

Brief mention has already been made in passing to boat casting. Some people are a little apprehensive of flying hooks in a confined space, and rightly so. Always exercise due care before making a cast. Boats regardless of size, create water disturbance. Couple this to a number of people stamping up and down the deck, talking , bumping weights on the hull, perhaps a VHF radio and a taut anchor rope cutting the tide, and that adds up to a whole lot of noise. Not that disturbance is totally preventable. Recognising its effects, and taking avoiding action is what it is all about. Even an empty boat at anchor creates noise. Imagine a large stone lying on a shallow river bed. Some way down stream, a small 'boil' occurs as deflected water is angled upwards. Now imagine the same idea in reverse, only this time a boat hull is deflecting water downwards as the tide pushes past. Given that the sea is shallow enough, somewhere down tide an area of disturbance is set up. In addition, throw in a few other nasty vibrations, and is it any wonder fish get the frighteners on? Not that all fish react in like manner. Bass for example give undefined disturbances a wide berth. Flatties on the other hand couldn't give a hoot. Obviously, as water depth increases, so the deterrent effect diminishes. Our problem is that many species of fish see a need to be in water so shallow as to become boat shy. Fortunately, human nature being what it is, where problems exist always there is someone willing to try and sort them out. In this instance we have John Rawle and Bob Cox from Bradwell to thank.

Water disturbance is not viewed by fish as a stone wall, merely an obstacle in the way of direct swimming. In short, from a point some way down tide, they begin to give the boat a wide berth. As straight down lines are for the most part fishing barren water, Rawle and Cox set about intercepting these fish, and to great effect with some huge catches from water often no deeper than six feet. By casting breakaway leads uptide, then allowing them to roll a little before digging in, they found that baits could be cast and held anywhere. Obviously, it is not quite as simple as that. Nothing good ever comes too easily. To keep the weight in place, a line belly must be allowed to form; monofilament of low breaking strain offers the least water resistance, hence a need for less weight. Tighten up the line and the lead

(continued on page 134)

Terminal Tackle Set-ups

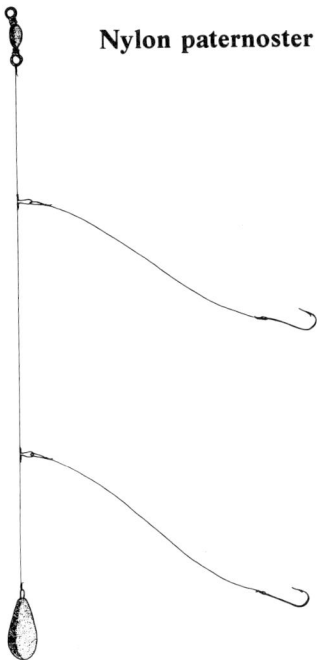

Nylon paternoster

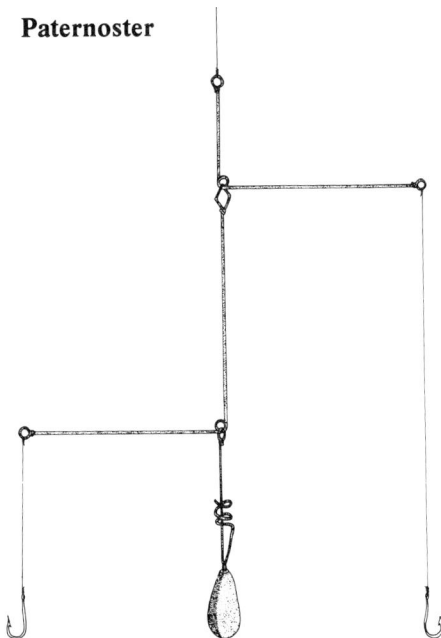

Paternoster

Redgill trolling rig

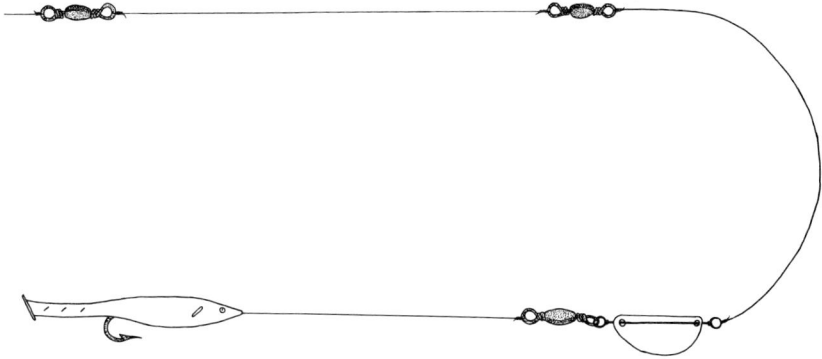

Flowing trace

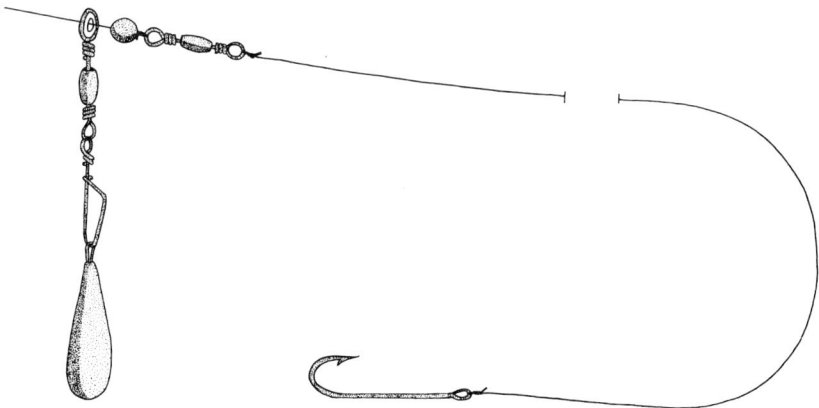

French boom

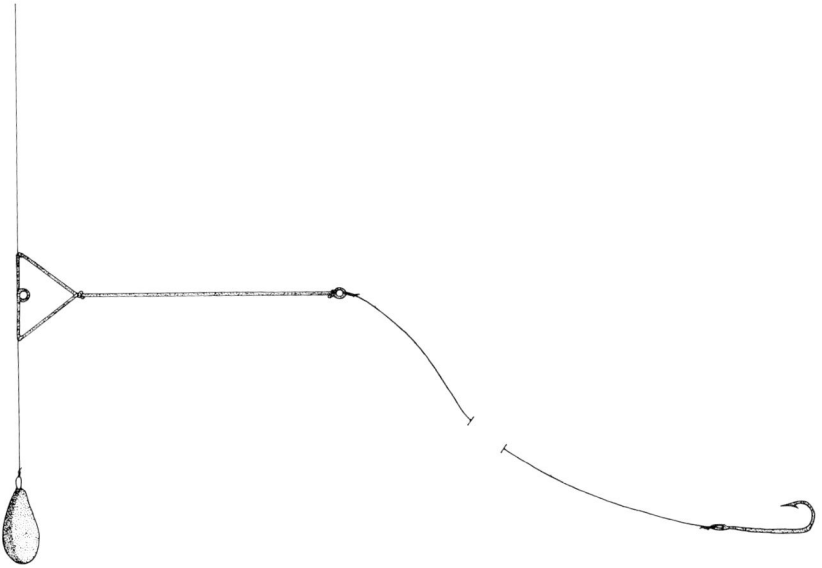

Flying collar

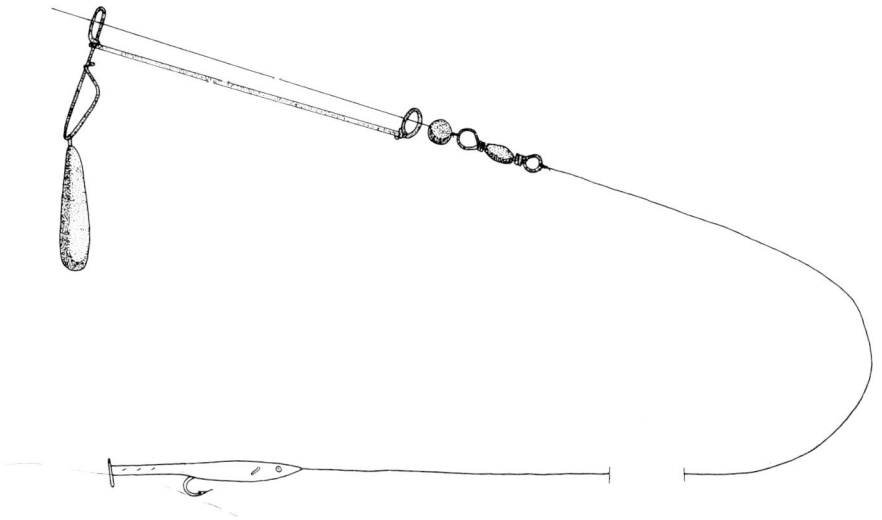

Mackerel feathers

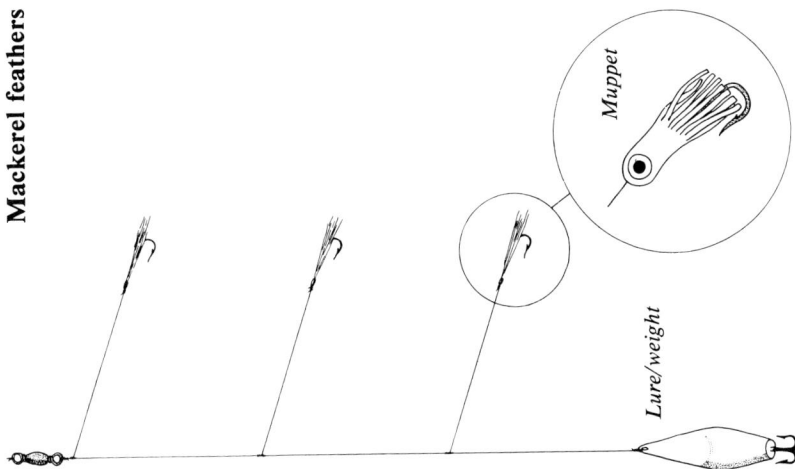

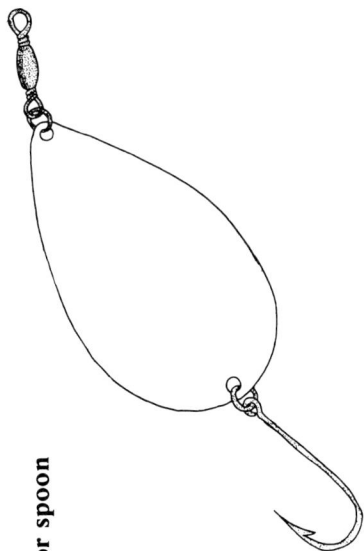

Muppet

Lure/weight

Attractor spoon

Flounder spoon

simply jumps its hold. Bites show either conventionally, or by themselves dislodging the breakaway. Reaction to the bites is where the key to either failure or success lies. Whatever else you might be tempted to do, fighting that urge to strike is an absolute must, for it will be a complete waste of time. All that happens is that some of the line belly is pulled straight. Instead, wind like fury until you feel the weight of the fish, then drive the hook home hard. Of course, if your line is trotted astern, it is business as usual, which is the position most small boaters find themselves in. The ability to fish across, or uptide, is always handy for days when too many rods clutter the transom. Not an essential technique for dinghy fishing, but well worth understanding, as is the fact that all boats, regardless of size, can put the dampeners on inshore feeding fish.

Hooking a fish is one thing, getting it on board is often quite another problem. I was led to believe that the thrill in angling is that long-awaited fish on the end of your line. Why then, the instant the connection is made, many people go to pieces, defies all explanation. When that fish hits surface, there will not be a more risky period, yet this is where most relationships go totally wrong. As a diver, I can understand the trauma a fish goes through breaking the surface. On top of that, suddenly gulping in mouthfuls of fresh air only adds to the shock. Anglers too start gulping the air in. Nerves are on edge at both ends of the line. This is where cool, calculating experience shows. Often the angler is the first to crack, especially when his fish is a big one, leading to the committing of some of the worst errors imaginable. It is fear of losing a fish that will ultimately lead to this happening. First job is to ensure the reel drag is not over-tight, maintaining pressure to the spool with the thumb. This way, should the fish make a sudden dart for the bottom, it can do so taking line with it. Try whenever possible to avoid the fish breaking surface too soon as movement is more restricted in water than in air. Sudden unrestricted head shaking can throw a light hook hold. Now all that remains is the actual lift.

Small fish are no problem. Hand lifting by the trace, or a small landing net work equally well. Where more care is needed two main options exist, these being nets and gaffs. Back in the conger account we argued a case for carrying both. This does not imply an equal love of both. We use big landing nets a good ninety-nine per cent of the time. Our dislike of gaffs comes not from a moralistic viewpoint, although that could be argued, but more out of realism. In the hands of an expert a gaff is an extremely efficient angling aid. Put into the hands of a novice, you must expect to lose fish, leading to more damage than good. Damage to fish either destined for release, or those that escape, is unforgivable. Worse still, literally knocking good fish off the hook after all the waiting and trouble can reduce grown men to tears. So how does one become efficient? The simple answer is by practice, in the accepted knowledge that lessons learned might come the hard way. Put the 'hook' under your fish's head, holding the handle vertical. A short jerk, allied to the fish's own body weight acting downwards by gravity is all it takes. Wild lashing is out. Now keep the lift coming steadily, and over into the boat. Of course, theory is not always as good in practice. Try sticking the thing into a small lively conger. Brian once had one spiral so hard on the gaff that it unscrewed the head and was gone.

Netting big fsh can be equally hazardous, the pair of us both having experiences to quote. Brian's father Bob played out a cod of at least thirty pounds, only to find it would not fit into the waiting net. Fat as stuffed pigs, the things won't bend and fall inside. In this particular instance, both head and shoulders were still hanging over the rim. It is easy with hindsight to offer suggestions. At the time it called for rapid action. Brian lifted while Bob attempted to hold the head with his line. Needless to say, his line parted. That sudden slumped weight across the rim spun the whole thing round evicting the fish, and that unfortunately was the end of that. Of course, I got the sob story and had to stand there thinking 'only idiots throw back big cod' while tongue in cheek trying to utter words of consolation. Two weeks later, my crew man Steve struck into a big cod. Up she came and onto the net. Did I ever mention that big cod do not bend? Well, if I didn't, I was about to discover it first hand. As I lifted the net, guess what, it spun and was gone. If you are thinking that it serves the idiot right, well just hang on a minute, because Steve had his drag set and was able to pump it back for another go. With my next attempt at lifting, it was obvious an action replay was on the cards. Nothing else to do but lean over the stern and gill it by hand. At 30½ pounds, it was a beauty. Cod of that calibre are fish of a lifetime. No need to get a bigger net. On the next set of big tides, Steve found himself stuck into another. It came up in a tangle of other lines, all of which I tried to bite through, his included! Good job plastic teeth are none too sharp. Eventually over the net, I could feel the handle turning again, so I went straight for the gills. At 30¼ pounds, Steve was slipping! Now this lot set me thinking. Could lightning strike in the same place three times? I was not prepared to take that risk. During the summer I knocked up a new super net for jumbo time. A length of jointed stainless tube bent round bus wheel, complete with tyre, then jubilee clipped to a six foot wooden pole. The other lads found its sheer size most amusing. Looking like a trawl on a stick, I slung it aboard the following December. Garth Haslam had teamed up with me and was into a fish already when a bite came to his second rod. I struck at it and gave it straight to him as he parted company with the first fish. Seconds later, I got into a decent cod of my own. Eventually, bucking rod in one hand and super net in the other, I managed to scoop up Garth's fish. A quick glance, then back to my own fourteen pounder. With so much net surrounding it, my estimate of twenty-five pounds was, I don't mind admitting, way out. It in fact scaled thirty-eight pounds. Remember the proverb about he who laughs last? Well I did, and was still smiling until it got knocked overboard while disgorging a 24½ pounder for Ian.

We fully appreciate that not everyone is of a practical persuasion. Many would far rather go into a shop armed with pound notes and be done with the

job. Be very careful then about quality. Few shop-bought gaffs and nets are up to the standard required. To start with, many nets are flimsy affairs, looking liable to collapse under any better than average fish. Chromed gaff heads may look nice on the counter but it is a different story after a couple of months at sea. With the chrome peeling, salt corrodes the poor grade steel once encased within. Even with the chrome intact it is little better, as it cannot be sharpened for fear of the same. Then there are those aluminium poles passed off with both. Aluminium corrodes too, and they never look strong enough to start with. Even if the pole lasts, sea water may weld the threaded stud holding either head into a position of permanence. Wooden poles and jubilee clips take some bettering. An eight foot length of copper, or similar non-corrosive three-eighths diameter tube, bent around an oil drum with right-angled bits for the clips, will last for years. As for the net itself, either buy one ready made, or get a piece of light gauge corlene trawl netting. Gaffs on the other hand need a little engineering help. Try a local small firm, asking that they machine a point onto a length of quarter to three-eighths stainless bar, then heat it up and bend it. Failing both of these, or in case of dire emergency, gilling and tailing beats trying to drag fish aboard by just the line any day.

With your fish now inside the boat, some advice on retrieving the hook might not go amiss. Angling has long been in need of a good all-round disgorging device. My crew mate Garth when over in America found just the thing, a device called HOOKOUT, which, by way of our exposure in the press, is now available over here. Rather than try to describe it, take a look at the picture. Pressure applied to the trigger is uprated ten times at its tip. Those powerful toothed jaws are a match for any firmly embedded hook, even one deeply seated in the throat. Nine inches of steel separates jaw from handle, which is very comforting with conger, tope and the like. We used to limp along freeing hooks by all sorts of methods in the past. With the appearance of HOOKOUT, there seems little point in taking up more space. They come either galvanised, or in stainless steel, both with a lifetime guarantee. I am doing a great advertising job here I know, and believe me, except for two free samples from the States, I'm getting nothing for it. So I must think HOOKOUT is great. Certainly it will solve a lot of otherwise tricky problems over the coming years, or lifetime, if the guarantee holds up.

Groundbaiting was another subject mentioned, yet not aired. In essence, it means feeding small food particles similar to those used in larger portions on the hook, into the swim to both attract and hold fish. Minced or chopped mackerel thrown in handfuls over the side is at times successful, highlighted by the fact that many fish subsequently taken come aboard well stuffed with the bits. This is not widely practised, and for two good reasons. Firstly, loose feed both washes and settles quite some way astern of the boat, acting at times like a barrier past which attracted fish refuse to pass. After all, why should they? They don't know it has all been a costly exercise designed to shorten their lives. So unless hook baits are trotted well down

He who laughs last . . . Garth Haslam with his 38 pounder and the huge net used to haul it aboard.

A net made from a piece of corlene trawl used for fish even as big as rays.

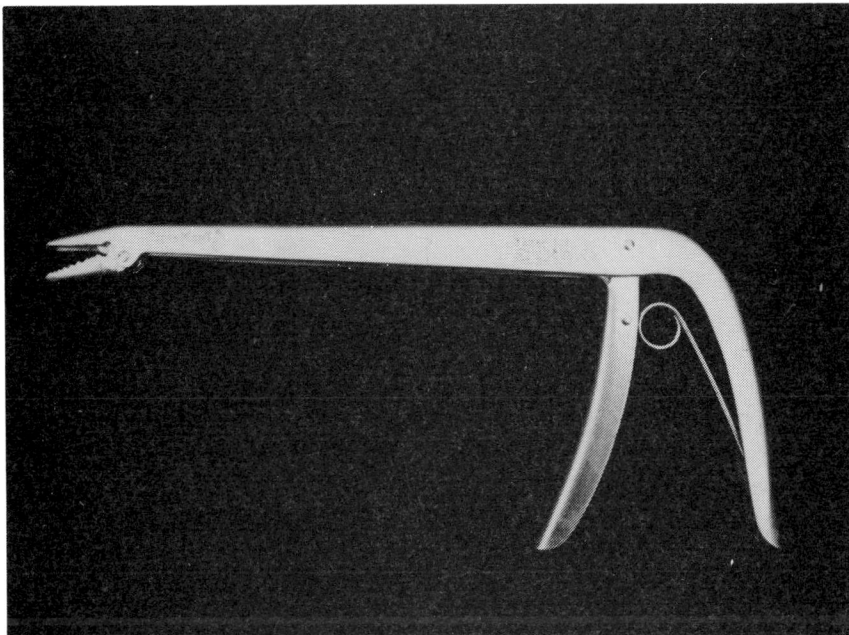

The hookout.

tide to settle on the carpet of feed, a reduction in fishing may well result. Secondly, in terms of amount of groundbait required, its cost-effectiveness rates very low when compared to more traditional mesh bag applications. Feeding fish munch their way through loose feed, terminating any interest shown the moment the supply is all gobbled up. Rubby dubby bags do not get eaten, require less to start with, and most important of all, draw fish right up to source.

The word 'source' is of prime importance, because thoughtless ground-baiting does more harm than good. It would appear the practice of tying onion bags full of mashed mackerel to the anchor enjoys widespread support. Given a perfect day, it can work well. Boats, as we all know, should lie in a straight line down tide from the point of anchoring. This being so, bits coming from the onion bag pass under the hull drawing fish uptide onto the baits. Any fish missing the hooks carry on uptide to the bag and are lost, which is problem number one. However, at least some fish are being enticed in. Wind with tide is an ideal situation we rarely ever get. Imagine a stiffish offshore breeze cutting across the tide. Fishing conditions themselves may not suffer, but the boat will be pushed out of position, particularly on a small or slackening tide, leaving the rubby dubby bag still attracting fish, but miles away from the new position of the baits. Beating this is easy, and makes for more effective swim feeding into the bargain, with a weighted bag attached to a short rope dropped over the stern. If the boat moves, it takes the bag with it, making sure no fish have any desire to move beyond the immediate fishing area. Moreover, it allows the bag to be readily retrieved for a top-up. On a swelly day, bits are encouraged to come free as the bag bounces bottom on its short rope. In calm weather, a good shake-up is recommended periodically. Onion bags are all right, but if any small meshed commercial netting is available, especially shrimp netting, go for that. It tends not to get all clogged up.

By this late stage, Brian and myself have done everything within our limited powers to see that you can negotiate the sea in both directions, picking up a few well-earned fish in between sailings. Now spare a thought for the fish themselves. With so much said already on the subject of conservation, people eventually become immune. Having had the plunder of the seas rammed down our throats in the weekly press, the decimation now of our coastal fish stock has long since lost its impact. Oh! we still care deep down, but more often than not feel either unable or unwilling to do a damn thing about it. Well, no sermon here; just a few words to try and point those dithering at the crossroads in the right direction. Conservation is not the same as preservation. Take fish by all means, but do so responsibly. What good is preserving if we never see the fruits of our labour? Let us leave you with one thought: conservation is a compromise made for the benefit of all, not an object lesson in self-denial. After all, who conserves the most, a man catching twenty fish and releasing them all, or another catching a hundred fish, yet taking twenty home?

Tight lines, and many happy returns.

Acknowledgements

Her Majesty's Coastguard Service.
Fishes of the British Isles and North West Europe by Alwyne Wheeler.
Practical Pilotage by Jeremy Howard-Williams.
Outlook – Weather maps and elementary forecasting by G. W. White.
Seaway Code.

As we would not expect anyone to either memorise or carry our book for reference, can we stress the importance of carrying an in-date copy of the new *Seaway Code*? This is a veritable mine of seafaring information, available from Her Majesty's Stationery Office, and is a useful way of keeping tabs on some of the ever-changing regulations, many of which we have detailed in this book.

Glossary

beam	width of a boat at its widest point.
bilge	the very bottom of a boat where the water collects.
bows	front of a boat hull which is usually pointed.
clinker built	traditional method of overlapping wooden planks.
compass rose	calibrated rotating inner face of a compass.
corlene	synthetic cord used by the commercial fishing industry.
cuddy	open styled cabin without a bulkhead.
D. C.	direct current as supplied by an accumulator or battery.
displacement hull	traditional design lying in and displacing water.
draft	amount of hull lying below the water line.
dropper	very short nylon hook length usually fished above the weight.
ebb tide	tide that is going out.
flood tide	tide that is coming in.
flying collar	very long trace used in the west country to catch pollack on an artificial sandeel.
freeboard	height above the water line of a boat.
french boom	a single wire arm to present a nylon hook length clear of the main line.
gross kerb weight	manufacturer's quoted weight of a car.
gross laden weight	weight of a trailed unit including its trailer.
GRP laydown	number of layers of fibre glass matting required to give a hull a pre-determined strength.
gunwhale	upper perimeter edge of a hull.
isobar	a line connecting areas of like barometric pressure on a weather map.
jumbo	colloquial term to describe a very big specimen fish.
lower water mark	distance to which a tide runs off.
neap tide	tide at lower end of the fortnightly cycle.
paternoster	device made from heavy gauge wire to spread more than one bait across the sea bed without tangles.
port side	red navigation light situated to the left.
resin rich	when resin cannot be absorbed into fibre glass matting due to over-application, whereafter it sets hard on the top.
rowlocks	'U' shaped fittings acting as seats for the oars during rowing.
rubby dubby	groundbait extruded by the tide from a mesh bag in the water.

slade	sloped concrete launching ramp from the road to the shore.
snood	short nylon hook length.
splash well	moulded depression forward of the outboard motor to prevent sea water entering and flooding the main fishing well.
spring tide	big tide at the higher end of the fortnightly cycle.
starboard side	green navigation light situated to the right.
stern	back end of a boat, usually with a flat transom.
strap conger	small conger eel, usually in single or low double figures.
trace	long nylon hook length.
transom	actual flat back of boat.
trolling	fishing a live, dead or rubber sandeel astern of a moving boat.